An Indispensable Youth I

HOPE
For The
YOUTH

By Osei Owusu - Aduomi

authorHOUSE®

AuthorHouse™ LLC
1663 Liberty Drive
Bloomington, IN 47403
www.authorhouse.com
Phone: 1-800-839-8640

Published by AuthorHouse 01/15/2014

ISBN: 978-1-4918-5017-6 (sc)
ISBN: 978-1-4918-5018-3 (e)

Library of Congress Control Number: 2014900483

ACKNOWLEDGMENT

One tree does not make a forest. Also, nobody can be an island onto himself. And wisdom, in all its meaning, could be learned from others.

Therefore, in writing this all-encompassing book, I have diligently researched into the earlier ideas and works of other writers.

These people have been remarkable beacons of guidance, encouragement and hope to me. My pioneer great thinkers and logical writers, I appreciate your rich heritage to humankind, with all humility and reverence!

The beautiful adornment of this book is the handiwork of Mr. Cudjoe Dela, who brought his expertise into the designing of the covers. I am very grateful to him!

Also, I appreciate the efforts of Jane Dadzie. She patiently and intelligently did the typesetting of the entire book. My wonderful lady, please accept my thanks!

I am forever grateful to my loving wife, Mrs Esther Owusu-Aduomi, for her financial and moral support. Mama thank you, and God bless you! And I bless my precious children, Dokuaa, Kwabena, Naana and Samuel for their prayers and manifold support while this book was undergoing production.

Now, let me mention Pastor Johnson O. Ayinde, the indefatigable and far-seeing man-of-God, and proprietor of Spring of Knowledge Complex Schools (Abuja-Nigeria) as my mentor. He single-handedly financed the typesetting of the original manuscripts. Pastor, God bless you!

Finally, I give my greatest thanks to God Almighty, who has brought a stupendous work out of nothing, and a nobody!

To God be the glory!

CONTENTS

PART 3
SELECTED SOCIAL VICES THAT AFFECT THE YOUTH

INTRODUCTION

God, The Omnipotent, The Omniscience, and The Omnipresent has given man a very powerful and sensitive behaviour regulator. This behaviour regulator is conscience: the unseen detector and assessor of what is right. Conscience has been described as "a wound which is healed by what is right". It is, therefore, not surprising that every society has standards and patterns of behaviour that are representative of what is right.

Also, He has made man the only creature with the longest parental association and care towards his offspring. In furtherance of this grand design of nature, every society is regulated by a set of norms and values. And these norms and values must be deliberately and constantly taught and nurtured in incoming generations with all pains. Here in lies the essences of this book-Hope for The Youth.

When a young person's behaviour does not measure up to these norms and values (society regulators) we describe such a person as a delinquent. He is often a wrong doer, either at home, in school, or elsewhere. Youthful delinquency (juvenile delinquency) is often the result of developmental emotions, drives, instincts or propensities which may not be very permanent. Therefore, the word "delinquent" is preferable to strong terms like dissident, anti-social, non-conformist, outlaw, deviant, and so on. There is always the hope of correcting this moral imbalance on spiritual and educational principles.

This is because the delinquent youth himself usually gives flimsy and very temporal reasons for his misbehaviour.

Some specific delinquencies are gender-related. Though they may be found in both genders, they may be stronger and more rampant with males than females, and vice versa. For example, females exhibit lateness, rudeness, quarrelling, gossiping and slander more than males. And males, on the other hand, are fond of stealing, cheating, wandering, bullying, fighting and uncleanness more than females.

Youthful delinquencies physically and psychologically affect the youth himself or herself (the wrong doer), other individuals, and the society as a whole. These delinquencies; if not identified and nipped in the bud can become uncontrollable social maladies. Remember these time-tested adages "The present is the key to the future" and "The younger shall grow".

If really the delinquent young grows without shedding off these delinquencies his or her adult life becomes a sorry affair. The blood-chilling life stories of hardened armed robbers, religious fanatics, callous cultists, selfish "pen-robbers" (looters of government coffers), blood thirsty despots and their likes reveal that their inhuman adult life records started as "normal" youthful delinquencies. Some of the vandalism, negative and unwarranted demonstrations, destructive protest marches, and general chaos in our organizations, campuses, in public and private organisation, are nothing but delinquencies in wilder and adult dimensions. The unprecedented wave of hard drug pushing and dependency, and secret societies' atrocities have their roots in what could be described as youthful delinquencies. Can we afford to have another set of social deviants, outlaws, and non-conformists now, or in the future? Certainly no!

"A stitch in time saves nine" Effective moral and spiritual education, and purposeful exposure are the stronger weapons against the negative personality symptoms discussed in this book. We must, therefore, deliberately create an educational system whose content and practice can effectively reduce or eliminate these negative personality symptoms.

Hope For The Youth, is therefore, a deliberate effort to train the child the way he should go, so that when he is old he will not depart from it. All hands must be on deck to bring the young ones to the knowledge and practice of acceptable, fruitful and positive norms and values of the society. We cannot bargain for anything short of this. Parents, guardians, teachers NGO's, doctors, social workers and all sundry, let's rise up to our responsibilities and bring up people who will create and maintain an orderly society, it is now, or never! The future starts today!

This book is not a product of a one-way traffic critic. Neither is it another sermon of a prophet of doom. Indeed, it is a balanced appraisal of who, what and where do we want our youth to be tomorrow? To answer these questions satisfactorily, we need to detect, scoop out, and examine the vices (delinquencies) that are the human nature in the youth. And we know that an empty sack cannot stand! Therefore as we scoop out the vices of the youth, we make deliberate efforts to fill them with virtues.

Thus, this book contains studies of vices and their solutions. I have intentionally set darkness (vices) beside light (virtues), praying fervently that the light will overcome the darkness. So, the reader should not be surprised to read about vandalism, lying, stealing, cultism and bullying alongside honesty, courage, temperance, tolerance, in the same volume. My goal is that, at the end of the day, the reader will know a lot about both vices and virtues. This knowledge will make it relatively easier for him to pick, nurture and defend virtues and at the same time expose, denounce and destroy vices. Behold, this day I set before you good and evil, choose what is good and have a happy life, the opposite should never be your portion.

May The Almighty God bless all those who will read and apply the contents of this book, so that they get the peace, tranquility, and success they seek more abundantly?

December 2012
Osei Owusu-Aduomi
Education Consultant/Youth Dev. Facilitator.
+233 (0) 547868396 / 206142810

PART 1

INSTRUCTIVE DISCOURSE ON PERSONALITY FLASHPOINTS AFFECTING YOUTH DEVELOPMENT

- Bullying and Fighting
- Stealing and Pilfering
- Cheating and Lying
- Gossiping
- Rudeness
- Vandalism and Rowdiness
- Truancy and Wandering
- Passiveness and Aggressiveness
- Fear and Worry
- Favoritism and Nepotism.
- Bribery and corruption.
- Intolerance and Negative Religious Fanaticism
- Xenophobia

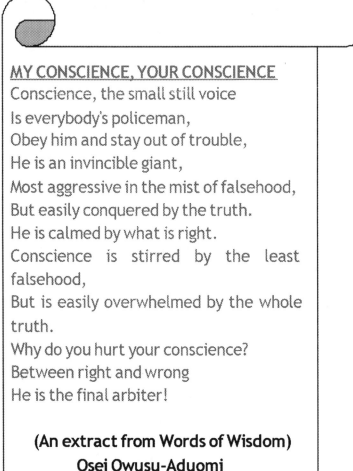

MY CONSCIENCE, YOUR CONSCIENCE

Conscience, the small still voice
Is everybody's policeman,
Obey him and stay out of trouble,
He is an invincible giant,
Most aggressive in the mist of falsehood,
But easily conquered by the truth.
He is calmed by what is right.
Conscience is stirred by the least falsehood,
But is easily overwhelmed by the whole truth.
Why do you hurt your conscience?
Between right and wrong
He is the final arbiter!

(An extract from Words of Wisdom)
Osei Owusu-Aduomi
ISBN 978-064-559-4

CHAPTER 1

BULLYING AND FIGHTING

The Nature of Bullying and Fighting

Bullying is the use of strength or power (physical force) to frighten or hurt a weaker person. Bullying and fighting may be used to get the weaker person to surrender what he has to the stronger or more powerful one. They are also employed to scare and chase away the weaker one from a particular place, issue or circumstance.

Bullying is not always physical; sometimes it could be verbal; oral bullying is very common with females and it is as bad as the physical type. It may take the forms of insult; teasing, mockery; cursing, taunting, nicknaming, insinuations and derogatory songs. Bullying and fighting go with aggression.

Causes And Effects Of Bullying And Fighting

i.   Curiosity and adventure may urge a youth to bully his or her mates. We often hear a bully say about his victim: "I beat him/her last time, he/she is big for nothing and not to be feared at all". With this in mind, he goes around 'prospecting' for victory over undefeated mates.

ii.   Idleness also contributes to the making of a bully. A youth who finds home and school boring could turn into a bully. To Him, bullying gives joy and excitement. After all, idle hands and minds make the devil's workshop.

iii.   Children who receive little or no attention (patting, commendations, approvals, compliments, encouragement, etc.) easily become jealous of their mates or siblings who do receive the needed attention. Out of jealousy they pour venom on their more fortunate mates for revenge. Also, such children may bully so as to attract the attention of their parents or teachers to themselves, even for their notoriety.

iv.   Bullying and fighting may also be a means of seeking redress. Human beings hate injustice and oppression, and they may bully others to "fight for their right". If parents or teachers rave, scold, tease or beat children without due justification, the affected children may fight back by pouncing on the weaker ones. This is an issue of transferred aggression. Thus, we see transferred anger in action. The bully often warns: "If I am beaten by daddy/mum, teacher, I will beat you in return".

v.   Inferiority complex induces bullying and fighting. The youth with physical and mental embarrassments: too thin, too short, too fat, too ugly, impaired speech, unintelligent, etc is often aggressive. He/She has a "somebody-is-laughing-at-me" mentality always.

vi. A child who overshadows his peers in age and physique is likely to be a bully among them. With such dominant qualities he will expect the younger and weaker ones to worship him always. He sees himself as "primus inter paris" (first among equals), and thus, becomes a dictator and a baby boxer.

vii. Charity, they say, begins at home. Children learn by imitation also, therefore, a child who sees his father, mother, teacher, siblings or peers as bullies or fighters may copy from them. "Like father like son: "like mother like daughter". "Show me your friend and I will show you your behaviour"

viii. Broken homes, disorderly schools and laissez-faire societies often breed bullies because they are the fertile grounds for other psychological problems like insecurity, anxiety, resentment, frustration and callousness.

ix. If children who have a passion for bullying and fighting are not corrected early, they may turn into sadists and despots.

Corrective Measures for Bullying And Fighting

i. Parents and teachers should carefully study the temperament of their children or pupils.

They should look out for quick temperedness, suppression, kicking, beating, teasing, insinuation, etc. from their children and counsel against then spontaneously and effectively

ii.   Action speaks louder than words, so parents and teachers should set good examples for the young ones to emulate. Adults should guard against any form of bullying and fighting among themselves.

iii. Equal attention should be given to children as much as practicable. Fair play, equitable love and concern, and justice should be the watchwords of all parents, guardians and teachers.

iv.   Children should be put in the same class or social group with due respect to their ages and physique. They should likewise be encouraged to form peer group along such characteristics.

v.   Children should be provided with adequate materials and physiological needs like clothing, accommodation, recreational equipment, toys and pets to eliminate petty jealousy, anxiety, insecurity, callousness and idleness.

vi.   Two wrongs do not make a right! Bullying and fighting should not be countered with revenge: merciless flogging or over-stretched isolation. It should always be handled with assertiveness, understanding, sympathy, and effective education so as to achieve reformation; but not to create an outlaw. Parents, teachers and guardians may seek help from elsewhere; preferably, from an educationalist or a psychologist when the situation is beyond their control.

vii.   When all methods fail God will never fail! Resort to sincere and fervent prayers so that God will reform the bully.

THINK ABOUT THIS

"Bullying and fighting may also be a means of seeking redress. Human beings hate injustice and oppression; and they may bully others to 'fight for their right'...

... Parents, guardians, teachers, are we free from guilt? We must address this issue positively!

Be a reformer, buy more copies of this book and give to your loved ones. In this way, you will help build a better society!

CHAPTER 2

STEALING AND PILFERING

The Nature Of Stealing And Pilfering

Stealing implies taking away from someone else secretly, without right and unlawfully, what is not yours. When stealing is casual and involves taking just small quantities of things, it is referred to as pilfering. Nevertheless, stealing and pilfering are equally unpleasant, bad and embarrassing.

According to Gesell (a prominent psychologist) the propensity to steal becomes stronger among children from 6-10 years. Stealing is more rampant with boys than girls.

Causes And Effects Of Stealing And Pilfering

i.   Normally, the childhood years are those of self interest. The child is controlled by the ownership instinct, which makes him a grab-and-gather being. He steals for ownership or possession.

ii. Poor and over-deprived youth often steal because to them, everything is new, exciting, fashionable, and worthy. Such children steal due to the fact that they have wild imaginations about every thing they see and come in contact with. Thus, a child may steal out of hunger and need.

iii. Oppositely, over-privileged children steal because they have an insatiable appetite for everything. Since they are brought up in the midst of plenty, they believe they should be in plenty always and forever. Thus, youth of wealthy parents can be controversial thieves.

iv. Children may steal for recognition and fame among their peers. Though the satisfaction these children get from stealing is not material, they stand out as brave, daring and smart heroes or champions in their gangs. They usually earn all sorts of nicknames and accolades like: "Fast guy", "Never Miss it", "Magic Fingers", Invisible Boy", "007" etc. These tittles are their motivators towards stealing.

v. Children may steal because they learn to do so from their parents, teachers, guardians, siblings and peers. As they see others do it, they believe, rather erroneously, that stealing is a normal business. In fact, in some societies stealing is so common that people are not even ashamed of it.

BE ARIGHT

Think aright and talk aright
Walk aright and work aright
Pray aright and play aright
Learn aright and live aright
Things done by halves
Are never done right
Yes, there are no short-cuts
To genuine and enduring success!

(An extract from Words of Wisdom)
Osei Owusu-Aduomi
ISBN 978-064-559-4

vi.   Stealing is a social stigma. A thief is a liar, an aggressor, selfish, and a person without shame.

Corrective Measures For Stealing And Pilfering

i.   Like all other delinquent cases, it must be handled with sympathy and understanding. The cure could be spontaneous and direct discipline. Stealing among young children should always be seen as a mistake and not a crime. Children should be taught public property morality. For example, what belongs to the family, class, society (the public) belongs to all and not an individual. Somebody's property is solely his, unless he willingly gives to others, etc.

ii.   Where appropriate, it must be punished with restitution, an apology from the thief, withdrawal of some privileges, and performing a task. Nevertheless, the punishment should always suit the gravity of the offense, prevailing circumstance and the average temperament of the child.

iii. As much as possible, children should be given enough of what they need (food, clothes, toys, books, pencils, money, etc.) accordingly.

      In some situations children should be given unfailingly what their peers have, especially in organized societies like the school, Boys Scout, Girls Guide, Red Cross Society, etc.

iv. Children should be guided and compelled not to associate with children who steal. They should equally be encouraged to frown at, and prevent stealing among their siblings and peers. Children should report all cases of stealing to their teachers and guardians.

v. Adults should endeavour to set good examples always. Adults should not only avoid stealing but also strongly prevent and condemn it among fellow adults. Children should, in no circumstance, be given the chance to witness or have an idea of stealing. It is contagious!

vi. Films, books, periodicals, television programmes, and drama that encourage stealing should be kept away from children completely.

THINK ABOUT THIS

Stealing is a social stigma.
A regular thief is aliar, an
aggressor, selfish and without
shame.

Dear reader, any better
revelation than this? What
should be my response, and your
response?

Be a reformer, buy more copies of this
book and give to your loved ones.
Inthis way, you will help build a better
society!

CHAPTER 3

CHEATING AND LYING.

The Nature Of Cheating And Lying

Cheating is acting in a dishonest way to get advantage or profit. Very often, one says what is not true to convince somebody else so as to cover cheating. Thus, cheating and lying go together. A child (youth) who fears to tell lies cannot be a cheat. In fact, lying goes with many acts of delinquencies, since it is readily employed to cover wrong doings by way of explanations and arguments. Though lying is a bad behaviour, it is better to let a child get away with a lie than to force him to confess falsely (tell a lie)

Causes And Effects Of Cheating And Lying

i. One of the reasons that makes cheating and lying common among children is that they often have false imagination. Often times children exaggerate their own feelings and intelligence and under-rate that of others. Thus, they easily cheat and readily tell lies to explain off their actions. They live in an unreal world: fantasy.

ii. People like to boast or inflate their ego. They do this to receive attention in the form of rewards and recognition. They usually find cheating and lying a short way of getting rewards and recognition.

iii. Jealousy may urge a child to cheat his mates and siblings, or tell lies against them. Out of jealousy children use cheating and lying as a means of seeking revenge.

iv. Cheating and lying are often applied as a mechanism for self-defense. When children are at fault and know that they will be duly punished, they may cheat or tell a lie to save their face and skin. Through cheating and lying, children may escape punishment, disgrace and disapproval.

v. Cheating and lying among children can also be as a result of sympathy for an offended friend, mate, or sibling. Loyalty and solidarity in peer groups are very strong among the young ones and they may go any length, at all, to defend and maintain them. Thus, cheating and lying are not always selfish acts, but a sort of relief package to others (selfless act).

LITTLE DROPS OF 419*

1. I want to be rich soon
    That's the road to stealing
    I want to ride a car soon
    That's the road to cheating!
    I want to build a house soon
    That's the road to fraud
    I want to marry soon
    That's the road to lying
    I want to be a chief (Leader) soon
    That's the road to trouble-making!
    I want to be popular soon
    That's the road to pretense!

2. A little stealing and cheating
    A little fraud and lying
    A little trouble-making and pretense
    All these lead to 419 (bad behaviour)
    Little drops of water
    Make a mighty ocean
    And little drops of 419 (bad behaviour)
    Make a mighty crime
    My dear brother, my dear sister
    Be humble and work hard
    Be patient to succeed
    Impatience and laziness lead to sorrow!

* 419 stands for fraud, pretense, and deceit.

(An extract from Words of Wisdom)
Osei Owusu-Aduomi
ISBN 978-064-559-4

Corrective Measures For Cheating And Lying

i. The youth should be made to understand that cheating is a greedy act, and lying can encourage one to commit all sorts of serious offences. Children should be encouraged to share things equally with others. They should be made to understand that life in every society is a collective satisfaction.

ii. Children should be taught to speak the truth always, no matter the circumstance or consequence. They should be made to respect and believe the saying: "The truth shall set you free", and "Honesty is the best policy".

iii. The youth should be told in clear language that false pride, false recognition, and false reputation do not last. They should, therefore, endeavour to earn recognition and reputation honestly. They should be ready always to pay a genuine price for recognition and reputation.

iv. Children should be advised and taught to defend a good cause. Lies should not be told as a way of showing solidarity. By so doing one may be held responsible for the actions of those they give such unholy loyalty. They should be taught that aiding and abetting illegalities and perjury are serious crimes.

v. Adults (especially parents and teachers) should always demonstrate transparent honesty to children for them to emulate. Our policy should always be; "leadership by example" Parents and teachers should always avoid lying to children or even to adults in the presence of the young ones.

THINK ABOUT THIS

"The youth should be told in clear language that false reputation does not last.

The youth should, therefore, endeavour to earn recognition and reputation honestly. They should be ready, always to pay a price for genuine recognition and reputation".

… "Honesty is still the best policy! Let's keep on trying. All hands must be on deck. It's now, or never!

Be a reformer, buy more copies of this book and give to your loved ones. In this way, you will help build a better society!

CHAPTER 4

GOSSIPING

The Nature Of Gossiping

Gossiping is idle, and often, unfavourable talk about the affairs of other people. It is the unnecessary poking of one's nose into other people's business. Gossiping and laziness are bed-fellows that discourage hard work and success. Gossiping Is a typical example of a gender-related delinquency. It is more common among females.

Causes And Effects Of Gossiping

i.   Jealousy and envy are the number one causes of gossiping. Young people (especially females) gossip with the aim of running down their mates and friends because of their special qualities, achievements, or possessions which they envy.

ii. Misinformation and a break in the communication channels (especially between children and parents or teachers) often create room for gossiping. This also happens between employers and employees. People, therefore, get the impression that there is something special they must know. They consequently, nose about for information, even at the expense of their school or office work.

iii. Children often learn gossiping from their parents, guardians, teachers, siblings and peers. They are often used as errand boys and girls for roumour-mongering, raising false alarm, and as baits for such mischievous acts.

Corrective Measures For Gossiping

i. The youth should be educated to avoid jealousy and envy. They should be made to understand that each individual is created with special qualities, and with hard work they are bound to have their own achievements and possessions accordingly. Children should believe in the adage "All fingers are not equal in length, but they are all useful".

ii. As much as possible all relevant information should be given to children clearly and in their true forms. And such information should be given at the correct time so as to forestall prolonged speculations and rumour-mongering.

iii. All mischievous information merchants should be brought to book and dissuaded from such acts. The youth must report all misinformation to their parents and teachers as the case may be, no matter the source.

iv. Children should be kept busy with adequate work, both at home and in school. They should also be provided with varied sports equipment and encouraged to use them profitably.

v. Adults (parents and teachers) should avoid gossiping to set good example for children to emulate. We should discourage gossiping in whatever society we find ourselves. Adults should not use children as messengers for rumour-mongering and gossiping.

THINK ABOUT THIS

"As much as possible all relevant clarification and information should be given to children clearly and in their true forms. And such information should be given at the correct time so as to forestall prolonged speculations and rumour-mongering".

... Who is fooling who with misinformation and disinformation? Such dangerous trend must be avoided!

CHAPTER 5

RUDENESS

The Nature Of Rudeness

Rudeness or naughtiness is very embarrassing and shocking; for it shows a total disregard for a person, authority or the entire society. Rude children are always stubborn and deviant. Like lying, it is one of the dominant forces behind many delinquencies. In fact, rude or naughty children find it very easier to commit many offences because they are immune to other people's feelings. Also, rude children are not often progressive in school because they are not polite and co-operative enough to attract sympathy from their parents and teachers. Rude children usually find it difficult to seek assistance from adults, even when they are in difficulty. Rudeness is common in those in the late childhood and adolescent age bracket, and it often leads to rebellion.

Causes And Effects Of Rudeness

i.   From 7-18years, the independence instinct in children becomes stronger. They would want to have their own way in everything they do and say. And when corrected or stopped from doing certain unfavourable things, they spark off in antagonism, confrontation, defiance and insult.

ii.   Inferiority complex may also cause rudeness in children. Self-pity, shyness, fear, and envy can compel a child to express himself negatively by being insulting, impolite, or disrespectful. For example, the complexes mentioned above may urge a child not to greet, apologize to, or answer his parents or teachers.

iii.   On the other hand, pride and arrogance that come from the qualities and achievements of the child make him rude and unsavory. Thus, superiority complex may also make a child impudent and unpleasant. For instance, children who are naturally talented in music, fine art, and sports are often rude; because they are always burning with superiority complex. Super beautiful and handsome youth are often rude people.

iv.   Excessive pampering, flattering and hero-worship can make a child lord it over others (his parents, teachers, and friends inclusive). Therefore, such negative acts do make a child rude and impolite.

v.   Rudeness in children could also be an expression against injustice. Children may be impolite to fight for their rights and legitimate needs. For instance, children often show rudeness when they are hungry or unduly incensed.

vi.   If parents and teachers themselves (adults) are arrogant, pompous, and disrespectful, they directly or indirectly teach the young ones to be so. Children may also copy rudeness from their siblings and peers.

Corrective Measures For Rudeness

i. Children should be persuaded (educated) to overcome their inferiority and superiority complexes without being rude or impolite. They must be open-minded, tolerant and forbearing, even when facing problems.

ii. Children should be praised for ego boasting and encouragement towards hardwork, and good behaviour; but not for self-complacency and negative assertion. A mixture of praise and positive criticisms could play down the propensity to be rude.

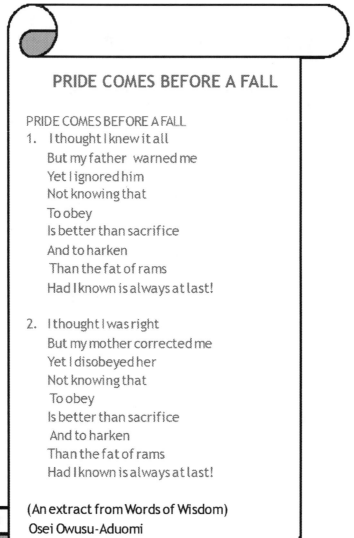

PRIDE COMES BEFORE A FALL

PRIDE COMES BEFORE A FALL

1. I thought I knew it all
   But my father warned me
   Yet I ignored him
   Not knowing that
   To obey
   Is better than sacrifice
   And to harken
   Than the fat of rams
   Had I known is always at last!

2. I thought I was right
   But my mother corrected me
   Yet I disobeyed her
   Not knowing that
   To obey
   Is better than sacrifice
   And to harken
   Than the fat of rams
   Had I known is always at last!

(An extract from Words of Wisdom)
Osei Owusu-Aduomi
ISBN 978-064-559-4

PRIDE COMES BEFORE A FALL

3. I thought I could do it all alone
   But my friends advised me
   Yet I snubbed them
   Not knowing that
   To obey
   Is better than sacrifice
   And to harken
   Than the fat of rams
   Had I known is always at last!

4. I thought I was the best
   But my teacher corrected me
   Yet I frowned at him/ her
   Not knowing that
   To obey
   Is better than sacrifice
   And to harken
   Than the fat of rams
   Had I known is always at last!

(Extract from Words of Wisdom)
O. O. Aduomi
ISBN 978-064-559-4

iii. The young ones should not be treated unjustifiable; parents and teachers (adults in general) should respect their rights and responsibilities. On every issue, care must be taken so that the young ones are not pushes to the wall; this will remove the right of the child to fight back rudely.

iv. Parents, teachers and adults in general, should be polite, respectful and show adequate consideration towards others (including children). By so doing the young ones will also have a model to copy from.

THINK ABOUT THIS

Excessive pampering, flattery and hero-worshipping can make a child lord it over other (his parents, teachers, and friends inclusive) "Whoever respects the great paves his own way to greatness"

-Prof. Chinua Achebe

....Who has failed in his/her responsibility? How, and when? All is not lost yet... But prevention is better than cure!

Be a reformer, buy more copies of this book and give to your loved ones. In this way, you will help build a better society!

CHAPTER 6

VANDALISM AND ROWDINESS

The Nature Of Vandalism & Rowdiness

It is the willful destruction of private and public property. If carried to a wider dimension, vandalism spoils the beauty of nature. Often times, vandalism is backed by hooliganism and rowdiness which cause panic, confusion and distraction from purposeful attention and focus. Out of vandalism the youth may break plates, window glasses, cups, bottles, pencils, pens, tables, toys, etc. They tear their (and that of others) charts, books, clothes, shoes, sandals and such things without reasonable cause. Generally it applies to mishandling and misuse of things, including radio, television, watches, clocks, handsets, and other such household appliances. It also covers the maltreatment and killing of plants (ornamental and economic trees) and animals (pets and wildlife). It makes the young ones destroy for the sake of excitement and fun. Vandalism makes children disorderly and dirty always.

Causes And Effects Of Vandalism And Rowdiness

i.   Lack of strict and constant supervision and accountability in whatever children do and handle may encourage willful destruction of things. A passive and laissez-faire home and school can breed vandals.

ii. Idleness and laissez-faire cause boredom; so children may destroy to create excitement and fun for themselves and others. Example`s are the practice of children hunting, (catching, maltreating and killing) butterflies, grasshoppers, and lizards. Children normally destroy willfully and unlawfully when they are not doing any thing constructive and useful (idleness). For example they break pens, pencils, shoes, or destroy other working tools to escape work.

iii. Frustration is also a major cause of vandalism. Children should, therefore, be helped and encouraged to achieve their heart desires and aspirations, as long as they are positive. For example, examination days often threaten students to result to vandalism and rowdiness. Also, when children`s play and work equipment fail to work as expected, they destroy and throw them about, out of frustration and annoyance.

iv. Willful destruction from the young ones may be the outburst against injustice and oppression. Children retaliate or revenge as a means of seeking redress. Usually, destructive demonstrations by school children are against hunger, harsh regulations and laws, and general deprivation.

v. Jealousy and envy often create enmity. At times, children destroy things with a view to punishing their "enemies"; those they envy. We often hear the young ones say; "If you won't share with me, I will destroy it" or "If I don't get it, then nobody will get it".

vi. Like any other delinquent act, the environment goes a long way to influence vandalism in the young ones. The youth may copy willful destruction from their parents, teachers, siblings and peers; either at home or in school. When they see people break, smash, tear, fling, kick, and knock down things and human beings without any justification, they are likely to embrace vandalism.

vii. Also children copy vandalism from the communication media—TV, radio, cinema, video theatre (drama), books and magazines. The so-called "Chinese" or "Action films" that propagate Bruce Lee or James Bond as heroes leave much to be desired in this aspect. They really teach vandalism.

Corrective Measures For Vandalism & Rowdiness

i. Children should be supervised closely at work and play, so that they do not destroy the things they work and play with willfully. They should be made to account for all books, toys, apparatus, tools, and sports equipment they handle. Parents and teachers should educate children on the need to preserve things for their own future use and that of others.

ii.   The young ones should always be kept profitably busy, at home and in school, so that they do not destroy things of out frustration. Those who willfully destroy to avoid work (the lazy ones) should be picked out for counseling accordingly.

iii. Parents and teachers should not unduly prevent children from using the tools, equipment and aids they need for their work and play. We should be fair and caring enough for children to realize that, after all, such equipment and aids are provided for their own good. There must be justifiable reasons for any embargo placed on the use of children's equipment, and aids. Such reason must be explained clearly, and at the appropriate time.

iv.   As much as possible each child should be given adequate books, equipment, tools, aids, apparatus, etc. so that he does not destroy those of others out of jealousy and envy. Children should be encouraged to share their property with others harmoniously. They should be taught the essence of inter-dependence.

v.   Parents and teachers should avoid willful destruction themselves. They should not destroy things out of anger in the presence of children. Any accidental destruction of property by parents and teachers must be sincerely apologized for.

vi.   There should be appropriate censorship of the communication media, so that children are not exposed to violent films and theater (especially TV and home video drama). Also, books and magazines that highlight violence and rowdiness should be taken away from children.

THINK ABOUT THIS

"Also the youth copy vandalism from the communication media TV, radio, cinema, video, theater (drama) books and magazines. The so-called "Chinese or Action films" that propagate Bruce Lee or James Bond as hero-shows leave much to be desired in this aspect. They really teach vandalism. Period!

Oh parents, guardians, teachers, social workers, governments, NGOs and the youth. Are we still helpless and hopeless in tackling this issue? No, not at all! Let's rise up with a godly zeal and backlist and ban all forms of violent media stuff! We are able!

Be a reformer, buy more copies of this book and give to your loved ones. In this way, you will help build a better society!

CHAPTER 7

TRUANCY AND WANDERING

The Nature Of Truancy And Wandering

Truancy is being absent from home or school often without any reason. It is the bed-fellow of wandering, because truant children often move from place to place to avoid their parents and teachers; at the time they are supposed to be at home or school. Truants are habitual absentees or gate jumpers.

Causes And Effects Of Truancy And Wandering

i.   Laziness is one of the major causes of truancy. Lazy children always hate work at home and in school and, therefore, are often absent whenever there is work to be done. In this case they stay away from home or school during work hours or days.

ii. Children often play truancy whenever there is a source of scare and unhappiness at home or in school. Unjustiable and persistent bullying, punishment, scolding, teasing, victimization, intimidation and general harrassement naturally drive children away from home and school. If he/she is sure of encountering these things always, he/she simply preserves his/her interest by being an absentee.

iii. Stubborn and insubordinate young people often run away from home and school in an attempt to have unregulated life and total freedom. Such young people usually refuse to submit themselves to legally-constituted authority. As they rebel against rules and regulations they stay away from home and school so as to be masters of themselves. This is a very serious cause and must be corrected immediately and effectively.

iv. Poverty and general need may compel the youth to be regular absentees and gate-jumpers. They labour outside the home and school so as to earn a living or supplement what their parents or guardians give to them.

v. In some cases some parents or guardians themselves encourage children to be truants for economic gains. Some adults find child-labour cheaper and, therefore, entice children away from home and school, with money and food so that they can 'employ' (cheat and exploit) them.

vi. Often times, children become truants through bad company. They learn this bad practice from their peers and wandering groups for adventure and exploration. To them wandering is fun and they do it with unflinching loyalty to the peer group.

vii. Usually, truancy and wandering become easy for children whenever there is lack of supervision on the parts of the parents, guardians and teachers who stay out of home or school for hours unending without any feeling for the loss of company (fellowship) as it affects their children. By this they are directly teaching them to find an alternate company outside the home or school.

Corrective Measures For Truancy And Wandering

i.   Children should be occupied with useful and interesting activities always. This will train them to love work. They should be educated to accept that laziness results in need and abject poverty. Children should be made to accept that successful work is the result of concentration and perseverance.

ii.   All sources of fear and intimidation to children should be identified and removed accordingly. Life at home, and in school should be friendly, lovely and sympathetic always so as to make children feel safe and secured. Children should be encouraged to be active participants in whatever goes on at home and in the school. They should be motivated to belong to the entire home or school without any doubt in their minds.

iii. The young ones should be taught to be obedient and submissive to constituted authority at home (the authority of parents and senior siblings) and in school (authority of the headmaster, principal, teachers and prefects). There must be effective rules and regulations, especially in school that make easy identification and follow-up of habitual absentees and truants possible.

iv.   As much as possible, parents and guardians should provide children with all their important needs. This will forestall the need for children to abandon home and school to work for their needs.

v.   Adults must desist from exploiting child-labour for economic gains. Government must make laws and enforce them against the abuse of child-labour and unjustifiable child neglect.

vi.   Children should be advised and encouraged to avoid the company of truants in their nieghbourhood or school. Movement of children must be effectively supervised by parents, guardians, teachers and social workers for them to be sure of their company, its motivations and destinations.

THINK ABOUT THIS

"Children often play truancy whenever there is a source of scare and unhappiness at home or in school. Unjustifiable and persistent bullying, punishment, scolding, teasing and harassment naturally drive children away from home and school.

...Do we laugh or cry? Over to you, my dear reader!
Are we still with our loving God?

Be a reformer, buy more copies of this book and give to your loved ones. In this way, you will help build a better society!

CHAPTER 8

PASSIVENESS & AGGRESSIVENESS

The Nature Of Passiveness And Aggressiveness

The Oxford Dictionary defines the word "passiveness" as follows "acted upon but not acting; not offering active resistance". So we understand that passiveness could make us fail to express our disappointments, hurt or frustration. We accept to suffer and die quietly without crying out. This makes one say yes for no, and no for yes; even when one means to speak out. And under such an insincere and confused situation we can only stand up for our feeling; desires or needs with the kind of timidity which makes the situation even worse. When this happens, somebody somewhere, quickly takes undue advantage of one's situation and forces, intimidates, or manipulates one into doing things the way it pleases him (the opportunist).

Aggressiveness, on the other hand is defined as; "quarrelsome; disposed to attack; offensive; pushing; not afraid of resistance". Jungle justice by which people angrily beat, maim or kill suspected offenders is the result of aggressiveness. Thus, we understand that aggressiveness fires us to reach our goals without considering how we negatively affect the rights, needs, feelings, goals, and self-esteem of others, by so doing. By definition we also agree that aggressive is the opposite of passiveness. But one thing is very clear; none of the two is a healthy human character! Is it not interesting enough to discover that the opposite of something bad is also bad? And how do we resolve this dilemma (or is it a complete confusion?). The answer lies in the middle-of-the-road approach to the two negative extremes.

Causes And Effects Of Passiveness And Aggressiveness

i.   In some cases aggressiveness may be the direct consequence of passiveness. When people take undue advantage of others' passiveness (excessive quietness, forbearance and long-suffering) the quiet-and-calm may explode and attack at unbearable levels. A ball thrown at the wall definitely bounces back; and the intensity of the reaction (the bouncing back) depends upon the force of the action (the throwing). A balloon inflated beyond its expansion capacity surely explodes.

ii.   As in the cases of bullying and fighting (page. (4)& (5), of rudeness (pages . . . (25)&(26) and of vandalism (pages . . . (32), (34), oppressions, marginalization, cheating, dispossession, blackmailing and general injustice definitely lead to aggression; which in turn disturbs the peace.

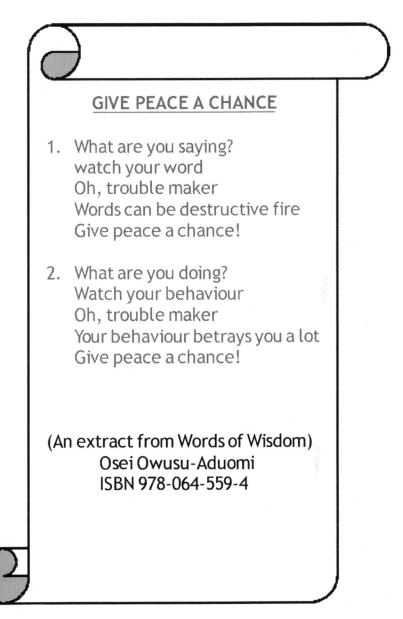

GIVE PEACE A CHANCE

1. What are you saying?
   watch your word
   Oh, trouble maker
   Words can be destructive fire
   Give peace a chance!

2. What are you doing?
   Watch your behaviour
   Oh, trouble maker
   Your behaviour betrays you a lot
   Give peace a chance!

(An extract from Words of Wisdom)
Osei Owusu-Aduomi
ISBN 978-064-559-4

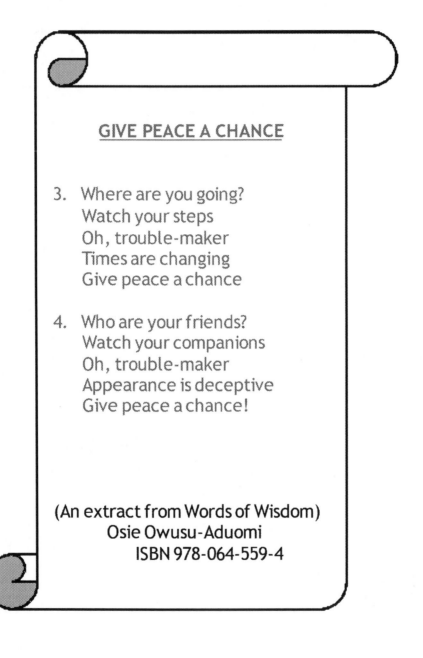

GIVE PEACE A CHANCE

3. Where are you going?
    Watch your steps
    Oh, trouble-maker
    Times are changing
    Give peace a chance

4. Who are your friends?
    Watch your companions
    Oh, trouble-maker
    Appearance is deceptive
    Give peace a chance!

(An extract from Words of Wisdom)
Osie Owusu-Aduomi
ISBN 978-064-559-4

iii. Intolerance and impatience lead to aggressiveness. For example, excessive emphasis on materialism leads to aggressiveness which in turn leads to armed robbery, fraud, rowdiness and embarrassing "gate crushing". Now let us consider specifically some of the causes of passiveness.

iv. Authoritative up-bringing, from the home, school, and peer groups tend to make people recoil into their shells. They fear or just refuse to speak out, complain, or explain unjust issues in matter-of-fact ways. Usually in such places parents, school authorities and group leaders use despotic rules and imposed disciplinary methods to cow their subjects. Even when they delegate authority to their children or prefects such delegated authorities are still total. The end result is obvious; their subjects are forced to live in passiveness.

v. Despotic political laws and rules may make people forget their rights and privileges. People who are used to military dictatorship, absolute monarchy, and communism tend to become politically passive or apolitical to things that may even negatively affect them. To such people their fate is in the hands of their rulers; no more, no less! They just keep mute and allow anything, at all, to go on.

vi. Religion is another cause of passiveness. The adherents of some religious dogmas teach and preach that total obedience, wholesale submission, and unbridled acceptance of every doctrine is equivalent to allowing the will of God to be done. The followers of such preachings and teachings erroneously believe that passiveness is holiness. In some cases religious passiveness leads to fanaticism which, in turn, breeds aggression, and finally completes a cycle of extremes.

vii. Some societies accept and practise the caste system. Under this system some hereditary social classes or descendants are considered superior to others. Consequently, the "inferior" class or descendants accept their fate as God ordained and, therefore, become passive to social or national matters that affect them even adversely. Inferiority complex becomes their task-master.

viii. Gender discrimination of any kind (religious, tradition or national) breeds passiveness of a negative order. Male chauvinism produces unreasonable discrimination against females (girls and women). Whenever it is practised, girls and women automatically become passive and suffer in silence.

ix. Ignorance, coupled with inferiority complex makes people to idolize their mentors or heroes. People, therefore, see mentor-worshiping or hero-worshiping as a normal act of showing appreciation. Self-imposed passiveness becomes the order. This is because any act of assertiveness towards the mentor or hero is seen as ungratefulness or insubordination: "biting the finger that feeds one". Examples of these abound in homes, government offices, business houses, factories or even religious fellowships; where political leaders, step-parents, guardians, senior officers, employers, supervisors, and spiritual leaders are seen as tin gods. Thus, out of self-pity, ignorance, and cowardice people impose passiveness upon themselves.

x.   Fear of resistance may lead to passiveness. The resistance such victims fear comes in the shades of misinterpretation, manipulations, accusations, blackmail, outright detour, and direct victimization. People who strongly feel they should not hurt others under any conceivable situation prefer passiveness to assertiveness. They do not want to offend any body and, therefore, suffer in silence. In other words, they want to please and win the admiration of all, at all times and in all cases.

Corrective Measures For Passiveness And Aggressiveness

i.   To avoid or minimize aggression, people must be oriented not to take undue advantage of other passiveness. People must not over-inflate the "balloon" beyond its expansion capacity. The safest policy must be "I count me, I count you". "Do unto others as you want others to do unto you!"

ii.   We must cry more for justice than peace; so as to avoid aggression. Without justice there can not be freedom; and without freedom there must be aggression. Remove injustice and you deflate aggression.

iii. Drama (live or video) films, books, magazines, and sports (judo, boxing, karate, wrestling, taekwondo) that teach or encourage violence and aggression must be prohibited.

iv.   Authoritarian rule, regimented lifestyles, and imposed discipline must be eliminated so as to reduce passiveness to its minimum level. Intimidation, manipulations, and jungle justice must always give way to consensus, the rule of law and mutual respect. "I count me I don't count you" must necessarily be eliminated. The rights and privileges of others must be respected, defended, and given, without any reservation.

v.   Religious dogmas that equate passiveness to holiness must be rejected. Voluntary forgiveness, as required by God, must be separated from seeking redress for injustice. Can a Christian (a very pious one for that matter), a Muslim (a very pious one for that matter), complain or go to court against oppression and suppression of his rights and privileges? I say yes! Emphatic yes! The God we serve who is also the Ultimate Judge is just, impartial, and very, very considerate in all His dealings with man. We must practise the justice, impartiality and considerateness of our Father-in-Heaven!

vi. All forms of aggression (bullying, teasing, insinuations, quarreling, fighting, cursing, intimidation, manipulations, victimization, etc.) must be exposed and corrected, or punished accordingly in all their ramifications. God is never a task master; and does not want anybody to suffer in silence. The judgments of God are forever righteous (just)!

vii. The caste system is primitive, inhuman and ungodly. It is a total affront to Gods highest creation; man. It must be resisted till it dies a natural death, the world over!

viii. All kinds of gender discrimination (religious, traditional or national) must be seen as undefendable evil. Male chauvinism, in particular, must be out-lawed without further delay throughout the world. Campaigns for equal rights for girls and women must be consistently stepped up till the female is assured a total sense of belonging.

ix. Ignorance is the mother of inferiority complex! Modern education and exposure are a cure for ignorance. Therefore, education at all levels must be restructured to overcome ignorance and inferiority complex. Education must never be seen as a meal ticket only; but as a powerful weapon against ignorance and inferiority complex.

x.   People should be encouraged and protected to speak the truth always and damn the consequences. Unbridled mentor-worshiping or hero-worshiping must be discouraged. To achieve this every individual must be allowed and assisted to attain his God-given potentialities. This will go a long way to reduce the timid and beggarly attitudes of people. We must teach, practise, nurture, and defend the "I count me I count you" policy.

xi.   "A coward dies many times before he is killed!" People must be made to understand that it is better to speak their minds and gain their freedom once and for all, than to keep quiet and suffer for ever! After all, plain word is never a cheat or an offence! People must be protected to speak out against injustice irrespective of from whom, where, when, and why we meet it. Injustice is just unjust, period!

xii.   God-fatherism in the home, religious fellowship, school, business environment, and politics must be thrown to hell without any bickering, whatsoever! Nobody should be cajoled to kowtow anybody! Basically, people should consider others as God-created human beings who have soul, spirit and body!

THINK ABOUT THIS

"Religious dogmas that equate passiveness to holiness must be rejected. Voluntary forgiveness, as required by God, must be separated from seeking redress for injustice."

.......Passiveness is a time-bomb. It is an unsafe safety measure; just that!

Be a reformer, buy more copies of this book and give to your loved ones. In this way, you will help build a better society!

CHAPTER 9

FEAR AND WORRY

The Nature Of Fear And Worry

Fear and worry are negative emotions! They can trigger off all sort of evil actions and reactions, with grave attendant consequences. Though the reflex actions may help us to preserve our lives and property; this chapter dwells more on fear as a flash-point in human development. Fear and worry are bed-fellows that have very strong affinity for each other. When fear gets hold of a person, that person ends up worrying. And when worry rages through the mind of a person and holds her/him captive, she/he becomes afraid of everything; including herself/himself. Fear has been defined as "the bad feeling that you have when you are in danger" or "the feeling you have that something bad might happen". From these two definitions; it is crystal clear that fear is either real or imagined. Psychological investigations have proven that fear that thrives on imaginations (fear that dwells on anticipation) constitutes eighty percent (80%) of all fears that confront mankind. This shows that fear that is motivated by real danger is only twenty out of hundred (20%). Therefore, it is not worthwhile subjecting yourself to fear.

Worry is the accomplice of fear. Worry is defined as "the thought about unpleasant things that might happen" or "the thought about problems that you have". Therefore, worrying is not the same as planning and solving problems. Most of what people consider as problems tend out not be problems, at all. They are often the turning points of life; the stepping stones to what we want to get, and where we want to be. Thus; worry is wild mental wandering about non-existing problems and anxiety over what is not ultimately harmful or unpleasant. It is an unjustifiable fretting of self; trying to imagine and solve problems of tomorrow. Surprisingly, fear and worry control, the lives of majority of humans; especially the youth. They torment, mesmerize, intimidate them; and finally rob them of their God given possessions.

Causes Of Fear And Worry

i.   The number one cause of fear and worry is sin and wickedness. People's past and present evil deeds do hunt them, so their good conscience breaks down, and the bad conscience goes into hiding, then, fear and worry finally fill the vacuum.

DOUBT YOUR DOUBTS

Doubts are bullies
Whose stock-in-trade
Are make-believe dangers
Doubts always bully you into fear
And make you weak and feeble
Only to recoil into your shell
So that you dare not come out
To harness your God-given potentials
And while you are caged in fear
Failure, shame, misery
Destitution, worry and stagnation
All torment you, all day
Oh no! Doubts are bullies!

But if you will brave doubts
And set your face against them
With all determination and faith
You ignore them with all impunity
And damn the consequences
Surely, you doubt your doubts
You will uncover their nakedness
As cowards who live on empty tricks
Then, you ride higher and higher over them
To possess the success you never had
Yes, doubts are the mirage of life
And surely
They will fizzle out of your life
Oh, doubt your doubts
And free yourself forever!

(An extract from Words of Wisdom)
Osei Owusu-Aduomi
ISBN 978-064-559-4

ii. Over-ambition for educational or professional attainments and success can cause people to fear and worry. In trying to answer the questions of "Can it be?", "How?", "When?", and "Why?" about academics success, a person may be possessed by fear and worry

iii. Choosing or accepting a partner in marriage is another cause of fear and worry. The speculations for an idle future wife or husband could degenerate into heart-biting fear and worry

iv. Personal hardship, failure, and disappointments do throw people into the web of fear and worry. People fret themselves because of the real experiences these setbacks or their anticipated occurrences may cause them.

v. Ill-health (prolonged sickness and diseases) with its characteristic kill-joy is always a dreadful monster. In normal circumstances nobody wants to be sick or dead. Whenever symptoms of disease and danger-signs of death become manifest, there is always high incidence of fear and worry. The strongest of persons become jittery when they directly or indirectly face disease or death.

vi. Closely linked to the cause mentioned above is the possibility or occurrence of accident. Accidents may, or may not lead to death. However, the possibility of an accident occurring often casts dark shadow on many people. They go through routine activities in the home, offices, factories, farms and transport vehicles with heavy fear and worry hanging over them.

vii. The atrocities of known and unknown enemies are major causes of fear and worry in people. When people consider what enemies have done in the past, and are doing presently to others and themselves, they imagine what they will do to them in the future. Such an imagination whether real or unreal, is nothing but fear and worry.

viii. Impatience is another cause of fear and worry. When people cannot wait for, or go through the normal process of getting what they want, or where they want to be, they lose hope of success. A common reaction to such a situation is to fear and worry. People who are used to quick solutions to problems easily become afraid and worried; whenever there is need to wait a little longer.

NO EXCUSE:
YES, YOU CAN!

No, I can't do it
It's very difficult
Nobody has done it before
It's going to take many years
And I have no money
No good education
No strong connections
And I don't have anybody to help me
I will not waste my time trying

     Stop!
     Look up!
     Yes, you can!
     Ask God to help you
     For with God
     Nothing shall be impossible!

(An extract from Words of Wisdom)
O. O. Aduomi
ISBN 978-064-559-4

ix. Child up-bringing is a responsibility fraught with fear and worry. Many people have fear and worry not for their sake, but for their children or wards. If parents and guardians do not see their wards or children behaving exactly as they do, such parents become afraid and worried. To them, as long as the likes, dislikes, passions, favourite choices, attractions, and distractions of their children and wards are different from theirs, they have enough problems to fear and worry about.

x. Academics and intellectuals often go by empirical facts and figures. Such data or statistics, as they call them, at times, reveal shocking and worrisome future predictions about epidemics, changes in weather, human behavioural trends, world and societal peace, environmental degradation; energy, food and economic shortages. For example, the Malthusian Theory and present day technological products reveal some facts and figures that induce fear and worry. The danger posed by thousands of kilogrammes of highly toxic chemicals embedded in hundreds of thousands of abandoned computers and other high-tech devices are enough to give someone sleepless day and night. This is a cause for fear and worry.

xi. Politics and economics, at home and abroad are highly contagious projections. International pacts and treaties of political economy; regional groupings and globalization reveal inherent fear and worry that do not only border national leaders, but the masses also at home and aboard. Leaders often hold meetings and conferences for hours unending, because of fear and worry. Business failure, take-over, mergers, amalgamations, and expansion create fear and worry that put executives and their workers on their toes.

xii.   Fear and worry are as old as human existence. Since Adam and Eve exhibited fear and worry during their living I the Garden of Eden, we may conclude that these destructive emotions are innate. Just as we say "to err is human" we may as well say "to fear and worry is human". Thus, people fear and worry about practically everything. For example, people have phobia about rainfall, winds, crowd, flying, noise, quietness, darkness, loneliness, animals, insects, colours, sounds, fat people, short people, tall people, thin people, sick people, dead people, blood, strangers, and . . .

xiii. Another cause of fear and worry is the concept of life-after-death. The starting point for this fear and worry is the ever-present phenomenon of death. People are afraid and worried because death will separate them from their parents, wives, husbands, siblings children, friends, business, property, money, comfortable living, lofty positions and even good brethren in the church or mosque. There are always the questions "How will I feel in the coffin or grave?" Where will I be buried?" "Will so-and-so be around to take care of my dead body?" Then, there are still the questions of "When I die where do I go to?" "Will I see the late Mr. A, Mrs. B or Miss C?" "Will I enjoy as I am enjoying here?" "Will I go to heaven or will I go to hell?"

The Effects Of Fear And Worry

i. Fear and worry are indicators that one has lost hope in oneself. The two giants say to a person: "you are a failure". "You don't have a Saviour, a Redeemer, a Helper, and a Shepherd over your soul, or body". Fear and worry interplay to make a person distrust and jettison his family people, friends, associates, and even God, his/ her Creator. Therefore, fear and worry are enterprises of sin against man and God. Since fear and worry destroy faith, a person who has them can never please God.

ii. Fear and worry create impatience and its attendant tension. This leads to destructive haste and confusion which bring about multiples of worse mistakes. Constructive ideas do not survive where there is fear and worry.

iii. Linked to these bad effects is the onset of despondency. A despondent person lacks interest, initiative, creativity, and positive action. Thus, such a person operates at very low energy levels that cannot break new frontiers for hidden treasures. A despondent person lives in a cage of inferiority complex.

Fear and worry make a person non-achiever; even a dead wood. Fear and worry never make a person pro-active.

iv.   Fear and worry inject toxic enzymes into the human body system which open it up to tension, high blood pressure, body weakness, and heart failure. Heart failure could easily result in the death of the worry-infected person. Fear and worry are deadly. People can commit suicide because of fear and worry about people and situations.

v.   When fear and worry-induced toxic enzymes do not succeed in sending their patron to pre-mature death, they leave such a person uncomfortable close to his/her grave. Many people who wear gray hair in their forties and exhibit mental and physical untimely-ageing are living victims of persistent fear and worry. They are on the "kill-me-softly" lane.

Solutions To Fear and Worry

i.   People should live their lives devoid of wickedness and sin, so that their past and present deeds will not hunt them. When a person has a conscience void of offence towards God and towards men, surely that person will have nothing to fear or worry about.

ii.   No man or woman can know all things about his/her educational or professional undertakings from the begging to the end, at any point in time. What gives the best assurance for our future success are good planning, hardwork, perseverance, and faith in oneself. When you have done your best, you hand everything over to God; and allow His good will to be done in your life. It is only God who knows your end, right from your beginning. You do not have to fret yourself over: "Can it be?, How?, "When?".

iii. Choosing or accepting a partner in marriage becomes easy when a person starts with himself or herself. You should always be sure that the ideal human qualities you want to see in your partner are first seen in you. A good man will surely know and attract a good woman, just as a good woman will know and attract a good man. To further eliminate fear and worry associated with marriage, people must "marry" good human character, and NOT beauty, prosperity, fame, profession, or social status.

iv. Life is never a bed of roses! Hardships, failure, and disappointments are bound to confront men. A solution to these 'downs' of life is articulate planning, followed by consistent hard work. When these fail, the best insurance against fear and worry is to develop a thick skin (a thick skin is not an I-don't-care-attitude) that can ward off the uncertainties of life not as complete evil, but a thin concealment of the goodies you are looking for in life. Never forget that diamonds are washed out from mud, and gold nuggets are buried thousands of meters inside the earth. It takes faith, hope and positive mental attitude to strike the goodies you are looking for. So do not worry, do not fear!

v. To avoid fear and worry that come with ill-health, it is very imperative that you should be health conscious. Plan and watch over what you eat and drink to eliminate junk food. (Refined and sugary foods). Find good time to rest and sleep. Maintain high standards of personal and environmental hygiene. Be vigilant and remove or avoid all sources of potential accidents at home, in the office, or farm. When it comes to the promotion of good health, prevention is always better than cure. If sickness and disease afflict a person, after all safety measures have failed, calmness and openness; not a cover-up, are needed to overcome. Finally confession of sins and prayer will banish fear and worry.

vi. You must get it clear in mind that you can NEVER please, or be admired, or be accepted by all men and women. Not all people will like your physical frame, character, speech, the food you eat, your way of dressing, where you come from, et cetera. However, do not see such people as enemies. Do not fret yourself because you do not get approval from all. Each person is different from you, and the other person. Therefore, each person is entitled to his/her opinion about you. But if you see the disapprovals against you are genuine enough, then be bold and humble to make amends. If not, continue to be your very good self and forget about what people will say or do against you. If you really have avowed enemies, pray for them and then submit yourself to God, who is mightier than any enemy you have. If God be for you who can be against you?

vii. You need to visualize victory, positive results, breakthroughs, favours, and success at the and of all your undertakings. This attitude is needed to remove your impatience that often triggers fear or worry. Remember that good, precious, and enduring things do not come by chance. You should be able to slow down, stop completely, or double up your efforts as the situation may warrant; and still you get what you want or reach y our desired destination.

viii. Child up-bringing becomes a problem when it is not affected right from the onset: child training must start from the day the baby is born. This is not an exaggeration! Whether the child can talk, recognize people, walk or do other things or not, certain physiological, emotional, and psychomotor standards must be directed to him/her. For example, feeding times and procedures, rest and sleeping times, environmental noise, bathing and dress methods, fondling and sound around him/her and cuddling methods and frequency, potty training, et cetera, are some of the practices that shape the future actions and reactions of the baby. At the appropriate age, the methods, types and frequency of approvals (commendations) and disapprovals (rebukes) are necessary for a soft or hard child character. Parents must lead by example and never push their responsibility of child up-bring over to the school, religious bodies. or civil societies. Parents, train the child the way he should go, and when he is old he shall never depart from it!!! Pray to God with your children about their behaviour, health, safety and success in life and fear and worry will surely bow!

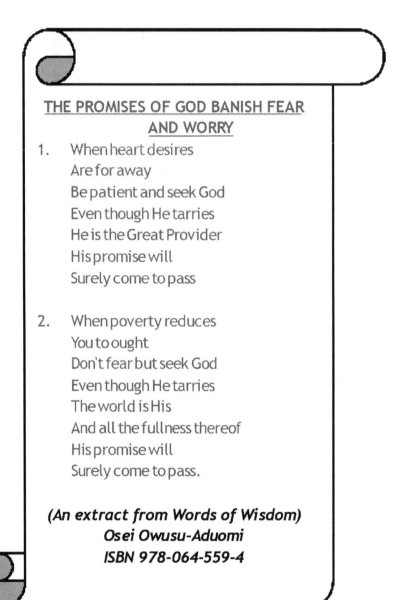

THE PROMISES OF GOD BANISH FEAR AND WORRY

1. When heart desires
   Are for away
   Be patient and seek God
   Even though He tarries
   He is the Great Provider
   His promise will
   Surely come to pass

2. When poverty reduces
   You to ought
   Don't fear but seek God
   Even though He tarries
   The world is His
   And all the fullness thereof
   His promise will
   Surely come to pass.

(An extract from Words of Wisdom)
Osei Owusu-Aduomi
ISBN 978-064-559-4

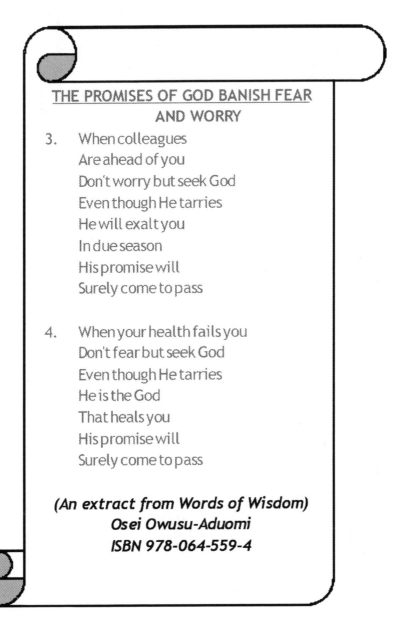

THE PROMISES OF GOD BANISH FEAR
AND WORRY

3.   When colleagues
Are ahead of you
Don't worry but seek God
Even though He tarries
He will exalt you
In due season
His promise will
Surely come to pass

4.   When your health fails you
Don't fear but seek God
Even though He tarries
He is the God
That heals you
His promise will
Surely come to pass

(An extract from Words of Wisdom)
Osei Owusu-Aduomi
ISBN 978-064-559-4

THE PROMISES OF GOD BANISH FEAR AND WORRY

5.   When all ridicule you
       And desert you
       Don't worry but seek God
       Even though He tarries
       He will sure come to assist you
       His promise will
       Surely come to pass

6.   When all hope is lost
       And death stares at you
       Don't fear but seek God
       Even though He tarries
       He is Life and Resurrection
       His promise will
       Surely com to pass

(An extract from Words of Wisdom)
Osei Owusu-Aduomi
ISBN 978-064-559-4

ix.   All horrible statistics, data, information, or whatever they call them, must not necessarily scare you. God has put in you, and in other people what it takes to find solutions to such blood-chilling statistics, data and information. Have faith in God! "When we reach the bridge we shall cross it", should always be your guiding principle to battle fear and worry.

x.   Rumours, projections and forecast about new reforms, elections, takeovers, mergers, expansions and business failures should not be allowed to frighten you. Why? Because as a human being, you are worth more than any political or business gain/position. Period! You are a soul who is wonderfully created by God, so He watches over your interest. Again have the attitude of: "When we reach the bridge we shall cross it"

xi.   Now, and finally, the phenomenon of death should be accepted as an essential part of our living on this sinful earth. The Good Book says "And the Lord said my spirit shall not strive with man, for that he also is flesh: yet his days shall be a hundred and twenty years". It also says: "Precious in the sight of the Lord is the death of his saints". So why are you afraid of death? Initially it is necessary to fear God because after death He has the final power to cast you into hell fire, if you are not saved; or accept you in

Heaven, if you are saved Therefore, you should be afraid to commit sin and worry about sinful practices and encourage others to follow suit. It is a happy and glorious thing to die as a holy man or woman and go to live with God, Himself. "O death where is thy sting? O grave, where is thy victory? The sting of death is sin.

THINK ABOUT THIS

Fear and worry are indications that one has lost hope in oneself. The two evil giants say to a person: 'You are a failure; you don't have a Saviour, a Redeemer, a Helper, and a Shepherd over your soul and body'. Fear and worry interplay to make a person distrust and jettison his family people, friends, associates and even God, his/her Creator"…

… Who says fear and worry are unstoppable? You can send them packing out of your life today, through prayer!

Be a reformer, buy more copies of this book and give to your loved ones. In this way, you will help build a better society!

CHAPTER 10

FAVOURITISM AND NEPOTISM

The Nature Of Nepotism And Favouritism

Nepotism is the giving of special favour by a person in high or advantageous position to his relatives. It is a kind of discrimination, tribalism, and refined xenophobia. Nepotism is most rampant in the civil and public services. It is also significant in private business enterprises. In many countries and societies it has become a widespread cancer. In a given government ministry or department, it could be clearly noticed that a good number of the staff are closely or distantly related to the key officer(s). This is nepotism at work!

Favouritism is flagrant or raw discrimination. It is the showing or giving of more regard, help, protection, kindness, support, advantage or sympathy to a person or a group of persons than to another. It is as dangerous as nepotism, because in both cases fair play is thrown to the winds; especially where discrimination is not based on merit, but on selfish considerations.

Nepotism and favouritism are all based on partiality, but slightly different. Nepotism strictly favours relatives (either closed or distant) ; whereas favouritism benefits non-relatives as long as the selfish interest of the perpetrators is satisfied.

Causes And Effects Of Nepotism And Favouritism

i. Basically, nepotism is caused by uncontrolled family or tribal loyalty. It is true that naturally, every person has a special responsibility towards his family or tribe. However, this inevitable responsibility, when discharged at the expense of due process and other people's rights result in nepotism.

ii. Unjustifiable partiality especially when it is the product of xenophobia, causes menacing nepotism and favouritism. Fear of, and hatred for strangers or foreigners are dangerous seeds of nepotism and favouritism. The "helping-my-own-people" syndrome makes other innocent people suffer.

iii. Selfishness fuels nepotism and favouritism. People who seek tribal or ethnic recognition blindly may readily resort to nepotism. By so doing they deceive their people into believing that they, they the perpetrators are their "messiahs" or god-fathers. Another form of selfishness that leads to nepotism and favouritism is personal interest in monetary gains. In this case, people even show favour to their relations, still in return for money. This is a complex and very disturbing cause.

iv. Sexual gratification is a very stubborn, powerful and omnipresent evil that promotes favouritism. This cause easily bedevils both the males and females. It cuts across the poverty line, social classifications, tribal and racial differences. Sexual pleasure can cause blind favoritism and insensitivity.

v.   Nepotism and favouritism, in turns, cause low productivity in government services. As soon as merit is thrown to the dogs, mediocrity, eye-service, and general hypocrisy become the order. Square pegs find themselves in round holes; and the result is non-performance. To some extent, this is the reason why the civil and public services are lethargic and more costly to run.

vi. In the case of private business, nepotism and favouritism may cause low productivity, as well as high production cost and finally folding up. These twain cankerworms kill competition among workers and reduce expected profit yields.

vii. These social vices also create suspicion and tension among workers, students, and any human groups. Whenever appointments, admissions, promotions, demotions, and dismissals are made within the premises of nepotism and favouritism, they are greeted with suspicion and rumour-mongering. Nepotism and favouritism damage trust, confidence, and esprit de corps (team loyalty) whenever they are practised.

Corrective Measures For Nepotism And Favouritism

i. People must be educated to know and practise the fact that family or tribal allegiance and responsibility are never enough reasons for anybody to sideline or marginalize others. We must categorically denounce nepotism as an evil practice. No more, no less!

ii. Again, we must collectively expose and condemn xenophobia so as to avoid nepotism. We must never use nepotism to settle old scores with strangers or foreigners. Such a ploy will surely backfire someday!

iii. The age-old "helping my-people" syndrome is shameful and evil enough, so people in republican authority must stay clear of it. Republican responsibilities should not be confused with those of a kingdom or monarchy. A good chance must be given to merit, healthy competition, and pluralism. By so doing we can reduce and finally eliminate nepotism faster.

iv. Selfishness, in the form of financial or sexual gratification must be condemned and punished, no matter who is involved. This will serve as a deterrent to present and future criminals of this order.

v. There must be concerted efforts by government and the citizenry (bearing the greater responsibility) to resent, expose, and prosecute all forms of nepotism and favouritism in the civil and public services. All appointments, admissions, promotions, demotions and dismissals must be careful scrutinized to detect and eliminate any acts of nepotism and favouritism connected with such exercises. Preferential quotas for admissions, and employment on tribal and family considerations must be carefully examined and played down. Also, the award of public contracts and auctions must have a 'holy processing' (due process) to avoid these evils.

vi. Private entrepreneurs must be enlightened for them to realize that nepotism and favouritism deprive them of efficient labour which gives them increased productivity. They should be made to know that these evil practices could make the employees lose confidence and trust in them and they will in turn lose the loyalty of their employees. Employers must, therefore, remove suspicion, tension, and low team spirit by completely eschewing nepotism and favouritism.

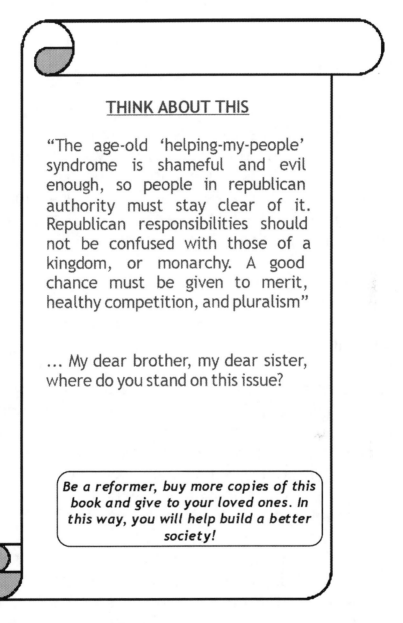

THINK ABOUT THIS

"The age-old 'helping-my-people' syndrome is shameful and evil enough, so people in republican authority must stay clear of it. Republican responsibilities should not be confused with those of a kingdom, or monarchy. A good chance must be given to merit, healthy competition, and pluralism"

... My dear brother, my dear sister, where do you stand on this issue?

Be a reformer, buy more copies of this book and give to your loved ones. In this way, you will help build a better society!

CHAPTER 11

EBRIBERY AND CORRUPTION

The Nature Of Bribery And Corruption

Bribery is asking for, giving or promising to give something to influence or persuade somebody in favour of the giver. The thing asked for, given or promised may be in cash or in kind. It may be big or small, valuable or not valuable, lasting or casual. As long as the giving perverts the course of fair play, transparency and common justice, a bribe is given; and it is evil.

A bribe may also be given to influence or persuade somebody to speak or act contrary in a matter so as to cover the truth, or unduly promote the self-interest of the giver. Also a bribe could be given to influence or persuade somebody to be silent or absent when he is required to speak on a particular issue. Giving of bribe is usually seriously frowned at in the public offices, and in the courts. However, people fail to realize that It starts from, and is most rampant in homes, schools and colleges. It is even in higher occurrence among young children and adolescents. Bribery leads to corruption!

Corruption in this context stands for immorality, untrustworthiness, dishonesty, sinful disposition, criminal god-fathersim, and general insensitivity to serious issues of life. In fact, examination malpractice, rigging of elections, embezzlement and misappropriation of public funds, are in the domain of corruption. A corrupt person easily says yes for no. He is essentially a person of double standards. He is unpredictable and, therefore, highly unreliable, any day, anywhere, and in any matter. A corrupt person finds it difficult to strike a balance between what is right and wrong. It must be considered that the use of foul language, excessive exaggerations, and criminally sugarcoated words are signs of a corrupt mind. Simply put, a corrupt person is a dangerous person. The giver and the receiver of a bribe are equally guilty of this vice.

Causes And Effects Of Bribery And Corruption

i.   Egoism (uncontrolled self-interest) and over ambition motivate people to offer bribe at the least opportunity. They strive hard to be ahead of everyone. They simply refuse to listen to and consider the needs and rights of others. They give anything possible to make mentors for themselves.

ii.   Self-gratification and over-indulgence are also causes of bribe taking. Over indulgence can make a person be in perpetual need of practically everything. Because of constant need, graft becomes the easiest way to promote over-indulgence, and bribe taking consequently becomes a normal way of life.

iii. Mediocrity and inferiority complex threaten people with fear of failure or non-achievements. Thus, people resort to brie giving as a cover for their failure and shortcomings. However, when they get what they want through bribery, that does not make them better still. Therefore, bribery deepens and multiplies mediocrity and inferiority complex.

iv. People who accept bribe do sell their conscience. They are never honest, straight forward, nor reliable. People avoid and even hate them. They are not principled; and can easily sell their birth-right for a morsel of pottage. Bribe receivers are often demoted, given out-right dismissal, or even convicted in law courts. It leads to shame!

v. Bribe takers always find themselves in a vicious circle of poverty. The more they receive bribes, the more reckless they become in spending money. They have the false belief that they can always easily replenish their pockets. Such people always live from hand to mouth; they wallow in unending poverty and hopelessness. They find it difficult to break even because they do not sow any seeds of progress; yes, bribe takers are never progressive!

vi. Bribe givers may borrow or even steal the money and things they give to receive favours. Whenever such expected favours do not 'materialize', bribe givers land in debts and other serious troubles. Any time the "deal" fizzles out they are losers. Again, bribe given does not solve problems, but rather multiplies crimes and sins!

HELL IS REAL

Hell is not made for nought
Believe it or not
It is a place of torment
Large enough to contain all sinners
Hell is real!

Hell is not made for nought
Believe it or not
It is a place for the ungodly
The wicked, and all that forget God
Hell is real!

(An extract from Words of Wisdom)
Osei Owusu-Aduomi
ISBN 978-064-559-4

viii. Bribery and corruption necessitate money laundering when they involve huge sums of money. Such deals put more liquid cash into circulation and, therefore, artificial inflation or deflation could be triggered. Artificial inflation or deflation is not a normal market force, so it becomes difficult for investors to predict and prepare for it. Thus, bribery and corruption, as a regular and prevalent system, can hinder investment in the economy. They are economic maladies!

ix. Bribery and corruption can stifle competition. When this happens, unfavoured investors end up paying more for their business or operate in a more difficult economic environment. Such a situation can lead to business closure and its attendant unemployment.

x. Bribery and corruption create a 'rich class.' Such rich but uneconomic class may direct their money power into criminal and destabilizing political activities. These evil undertakings are always inimical to national peace and development. As corrupt people become "money bags" on a silver platter, they command "cheap money" so they use it recklessly to the chagrin of the law-abiding and hard-working citizens. For example, political instability, illicit hard drugs business, fraudulent export and import business could be facilitated by bribery and corruption.

Corrective Measures For Bribery And Corruption

i.   People should be taught that success in life is not a matter of life-and-death. And that over-ambition leads people to bigger and deeper problems; and even outright death. Also, it must be emphasized, and re-emphasized, that getting ahead of everybody is not always possible. This is because "success" or "achievement" is relative, and not an absolute term. What passes for success or achievement today, in a particular setting, may pass for failure or loss tomorrow, in another setting. Therefore, irrational comparison with others must be discouraged. The popular "Is-he-not-your-age-or-class-mate?" mentality must be stopped. "Godliness with contentment is great gain. For we brought nothing into this world, and it is certain we can carry nothing out. And having food and raiment let us be therewith content. For the love of money is the root of evil".

ii.   Merit should never, never, be sacrificed for mediocrity. Merit should be seen as gold, while mediocrity should be considered as dross. No effort must be spared to honour and reward merit; but mediocrity must be discouraged always. And reward for merit should not necessarily be monetary. After all, money or affluence is not synonymous to merit.

iii. Bribery, and corruption are crimes, as well as sins. People must be made to understand that these facts (their criminal and sinful nature) are non-negotiable, any day, anywhere, and under any circumstance. Campaigns against bribery and corruption must never be a nine-day wonder. They must be sustained to every convincing conclusion! To achieve this, corrupt people (refer to the nature of bribery and corruption explained in this chapter); with soiled hands, people with chameleon character, dictators, and suppressors of the common man should not be allowed to be in the vanguard for the fight against bribery and corruption. Don't forget, it takes a good tree to produce a good fruit.!

iv.   Now, it must be stressed that it is always better to work hard and earn a durable living than to resort to "quick pranks" that are bound to fizzle out. Bribery and corruption are never sustainable life styles!

v.   Finally, the crusade against bribery and corruption must not start and end with the big shots ("the big fish") in top positions. Starting the fight against bribery and corruption at the commanding heights of politics, the bureaucracy (the public service), the police, the armed forces, and the corporate business houses makes sense, but it is always temporary: a shaky nine-day wonder. A continuous crusade against bribery and corruption that will be a habitual national orientation MUST also take care of the grassroots. It is a fact that these people at the top use the common man to perpetrate high-class sharp practices. After all, prevention is better than cure! Countries that have reduced bribery and corruption to their barest minimum have made citizen vetting committees (CVC) organizations of non-negotiable patriotism. Countries that are dying because of bribery and corruption may resort to the CVCs with patriotic men and women as volunteers.

vi. Self-gratification and over-indulgence must be detected, exposed and severely punished. Everybody must see himself as a "policeman" of the general society. Honest and patriotic people must be encouraged and protected to stand against bribery and corruption in all its ramifications.

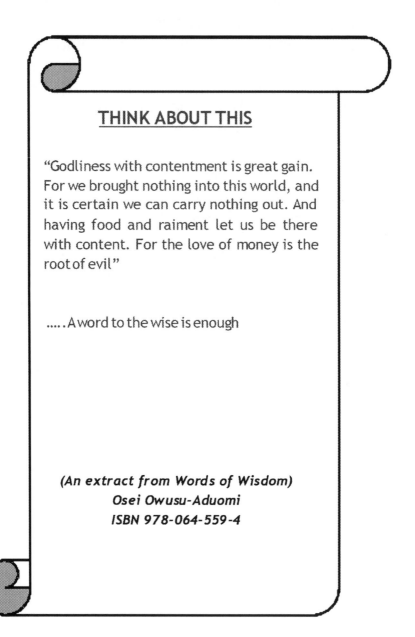

THINK ABOUT THIS

"Godliness with contentment is great gain. For we brought nothing into this world, and it is certain we can carry nothing out. And having food and raiment let us be there with content. For the love of money is the root of evil"

..... A word to the wise is enough

(An extract from Words of Wisdom)
Osei Owusu-Aduomi
ISBN 978-064-559-4

CHAPTER 12

INTOLERANCE AND NEGATIVE RELIGIOUS FANATICISM

The Nature Of Intolerance And Negative Religious Fanaticism

Intolerance means not enduring, not fore-bearing, not longsuffering, or being impatient. Intolerance will not help a person to allow some inconveniences without a protest. An intolerant person complains at the slightest provocation or inconveniences. Intolerance is a volatile fuel that propels anger, hatred, vandalism, arson and aggression. Intolerance could be personal, tribal, ethnic or national in nature. Any of these types is dangerous!

Intolerance is the bedfellow of negative religious fanaticism. In fact, negative religious fanaticism is a special dimension of general intolerance. The Advanced Oxford Learner's Dictionary defines a fanatic as "as person who is extremely enthusiastic about something". Enthusiasm is positive, and like passion, it is a human quality necessary for achievements. It is quite good for someone to be enthusiastic about his/her religion or beliefs, so that he/she will not be tossed about by every wind of doctrine (heresies). However, when it is extreme, fanaticism becomes negative and destructive.

In this chapter, we shall use fanaticism to mean the negative type. Fanaticism has been defined as "violent and unreasonable enthusiasm". So we see that a religious fanatic is always intolerant, not enduring, not fore-bearing, not long suffering, not considerate, not restrained, or impatient on issues his religion holds divergent views. Religious fanaticism is selfish, absolute, undemocratic and enemy of peace, the world over! Most of the world's most savage and long lasting wars have been sparked off by intolerance and religious fanaticism. No wonder, wherever they are found there is little or no progress, as the people lack peace.

Causes And Effects of Intolerance And Negative Religious Fanaticism

i.   Intolerance is caused by self-centeredness when an individual begins to say: "I count me, I don't count you"; then impatience sets in. Egoism (systematic selfishness) is the infamous mother of intolerance.

ii.   Superiority complex also gives rise to intolerance. When people think that they are always the best, wisest, most honest, most powerful, intelligent, most capable, most this, and most that, they tend to ignore and trample upon others with impunity. So we understand that pride makes people intolerant. Over-sensitivity and touchiness are signs of intolerance!

iii. Suspicion and fear cause anxiety which may give expression in intolerance. In the midst of general insecurity people find it difficult to wait, listen to, and consider the motives and actions of others. Anxiety motivates people to selfishly fend for themselves alone. By so doing they become intoler.

iv. When intolerance reaches madness dimensions it leaves in its trail horrible acts of vandalism, jungle justice, and general savagery. Thus, religious fanaticism is the product of intolerance. Infact, religious fanaticism is one of the most ugly faces of general intolerance. It is a terrible social demeanour throughout the ages.

v. Both intolerance and religious fanaticism lead to aggression. Clashes, skirmishes and full-blown wars are often the outcome of intolerance and religious fanaticism. Hostilities surely drive away peace, and since peace is an inevitable factor for development and progress, communities that witness intolerance and religious tendencies set themselves against the rule of law. Wanton destruction of property and lives create general insecurity; which makes any society stagnant and finally sinks into oblivion.

Corrective Measures For Intolerance And Negative Religious Fanaticism

i. Self-centeredness is a hydra-headed evil. It is the back bone of many negative human actions and reactions. No effort must be spared in condemning and teaching against self-centeredness in every practical terms. People must be counseled to understand that if they alone succeed in life, and have their own ways in all matters, and all others be at their mercy; their success and self-indulgence will surely consume themselves. Every parent or guardian needs to know that it is evil, and not love, to over-indulge his/her children or wards.

ii. Self-centeredness goes hand-in-hand with negative superiority complex. Therefore, superiority complex must be handled just like self-centeredness (see (i) above).

iii. To make people wait, listen to, and consider the motives and actions of others; there is every need to remove every trace of suspicion and fear from people's minds. In this way, tolerance can be nurtured and defended. Anything that creates anxiety in people must be gotten rid of. It takes sincerity, honesty, integrity, openness, fairness and consideration for others to install tolerance.

MY PEOPLE NEED PEACE

Peace must be
The purpose of my people
The prince of the place
Oh, a piece of peace
Is better than
Peace in pieces
Yes, peace must be
The preference of my people
No matter what happens!

(An extract from Words of Wisdom)
Osei Owusu-Aduomi
ISBN 978-064-559-4

v.   It is a good thing to encourage freedom of worship; any day, anywhere. However, people must be made to accept that their freedom ends where other people's freedom begins. And it is just humanly impossible to get all people to accept and practise, one, and only one religion or belief. Even though it is imperative for every human being to acknowledge and worship God as our Creator and Sustainer, He (God) never forces, intimidates, nor manipulates anybody. Neither has He mandated anybody to do so on His behalf. These are naked truths that must be taught, nurtured, practised and defended. God is tolerant and considerate, and so, His followers must be the same.

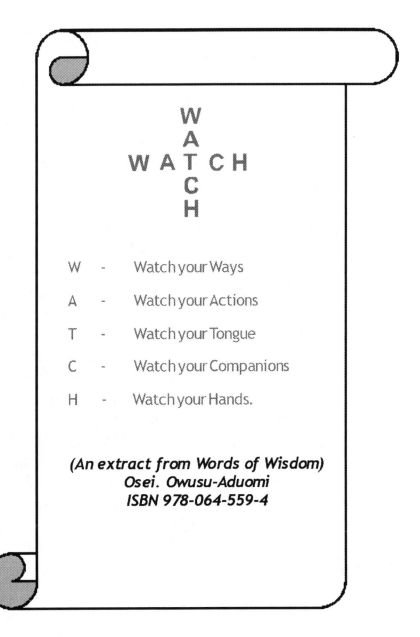

```
      W
      A
W A   T   C H
      C
      H
```

W - Watch your Ways

A - Watch your Actions

T - Watch your Tongue

C - Watch your Companions

H - Watch your Hands.

(An extract from Words of Wisdom)
Osei. Owusu-Aduomi
ISBN 978-064-559-4

vi.   People, who out of sheer intolerance or religious fanaticism cause destruction of property and lives must be made to pay for their callous deeds by the full stretch of the law. They must be punished decisively, without fear of favour,. After all, it is holiness (the nature of God) to punish willful and unrepentant offenders. Religious fanatics must be made to understand that it is profound wisdom to know that "Blessed are the peace makers and they shall be called the children of God".

vii.   Education is also a veritable antidote to intolerance and religious fanaticism. Education, in the form of exposure, interaction and co-operation goes a long way to remove suspicion and ignorance about other peoples motives and ways of life. Thorough knowledge about one's religion and culture will put him in an advantage position from where charlatans, false prophets and false messiahs could not manipulate him to be a fanatic. The right knowledge about God will be an eye opener against lawlessness. The idle mind and hands are the devil's workshop. Again, there is need for functional education that produces profitable knowledge and occupation for the youth. A knowledgeable and gainfully occupied youth will surely have no time to destroy himself.

THINK ABOUT THIS

"It is a good thing to encourage freedom of worship, any day, anywhere. However, people must be made to accept that their freedom ends where other people's freedom begins... God is tolerant and considerate and so, His followers must be the same".

... My dear reader, what is your verdict?

CHAPTER 13

XENOPHOBIA

The Nature of Xenophobia

Xenophobia has been defined as an "irrational hatred for or fear of strangers or foreigners". By this definition, we shall consider tribalism and racism as part of xenophobia. Therefore, in our treatment of this topic we shall use the word "stranger" or "foreigner" to mean one of a different tribe or race. Some people tend to feel uncomfortable when they see 'new faces' coming into their midst. They become withdrawn, reserved, irritated, and finally aggressive. In a lighter mood, such emotions or sentiments may be generally described as shyness or impromptu exposure. This may not pose a threat to anybody.

However, such an uneasy quietness, when fueled by irritation and resentment develops into a dangerous time bomb. In its explosion, distrust, hatred and aggression greet the 'unfamiliar face or the stranger. The end result is that the peaceful and friendly social atmosphere is destroyed to the disadvantage of all; the hostile, the friendly, and the innocent stranger. In some cases people see foreigners (people of different tribe, language, country and race) in their domain as uninvited guests.

The foreigners are seen as intruders whose presence is an evil omen to their hosts. This fear and hatred becomes rather fatal when they are based on unreasonable considerations.

Causes And Effects Of Xenophobia

i.   History is one of the strong causes of xenophobia. People who have been dominated, dispossessed, discriminated against, blackmailed and massacred in times past naturally tend to fear and hate the descendants of their adversaries, even many years after. Therefore, history of past wars, invasions, jihads and colonization may bring pain into the hearts of present-day generations; which in turn may produce xenophobia. I strongly admonish the youth all over the world to beware of such negative history. God will help us. A men!

ii.   Sheer ignorance makes people fear and hate strangers and foreigners. When people do not take pains to understand the reasons behind other people's eating habits, clothing choice, educational principles, religious beliefs, political system, and general culture they may irrationally oppose their ways of life. Rather than understanding and tolerating his wa of life, the stranger is seen as a non-conformist who must be eliminated.

iii. Other natives or citizens may not hate the culture of the stranger as such, but they take undue advantage of the ignorance of their kinsmen and portray the stranger or foreigner as a persona non grata. They do this to eliminate the stranger who they see as a competitor against their business, professional, political, or social interest. Such selfish natives or citizens craftily whip up tribal, ethnic, or racial sentiments for the necessary kinsmen-solidarity they need to crucify the stranger or foreigner with. They present themselves as "crusaders" against colonization and neo-colonialisation. But the hidden causes of their actions are nothing but selfishness, jealousy and envy.

iv.   Differences in physical environment, social and religious up-bringing may make some strangers or foreigners more humble, more enterprising, and generally more experimenting than their hosts. As a result, the affected citizens or natives may fear and hate the stranger or foreigner in their midst without any justifiable reason. In fact, inferiority complex causes xenophobia. A more gifted and enterprising foreigner is likely to be hated by his hosts who are less gifted and enterprising.

v.   Differences in tribe, nationality, race and culture are very important social and political identities. However, uncontrolled affection and attachment to tribalism, ethnicity, nationalism, regionalism and racialism (chauvinism and insularity) of any shade lead to xenophobia.

vi.   Superiority complex also causes xenophobia. When the stranger or foreigner feels he is better than the native, he makes himself insulting. Thus he opens himself to fear and hatred from the natives he despises.

Corrective Measures For Xenophobia

i.   The history of our societies, whether it is about our victory or conquest, must be seen as a necessary reference guide to build a better society for today. Therefore, people should see and embrace more of justice, reconciliation, forgiveness, peace, and reconstruction which history teaches; rather than pain, irritation, vengeance, and destruction, which are counter-productive. To err is human and to forgive is divine! People should learn to forgive their past adversaries. In some republican nations the component tribes and ethnic groups, still sadly, refer to themselves as superior kingdoms, empires, and even race.

ii. This is nothing but an ill-wind. Why should a present day republican citizen think that his fellow citizens are slaves or inferior to him because of primitive history?

iii. People must be thoroughly educated to understand and tolerate the different ways of life (culture) of others. After all, one man's meat is another man's poison! Such understanding and tolerance will surely magnify the good in other people's (strangers or foreigners) culture; and at the same time, marginalize the bad aspects.

iv. The human factor is the most important input for life on this earth. Fear and hatred for human migration is, therefore, the worst enemy of civilization. People must be made to understand that the discovery and exploitation of money-spinning minerals, detailed knowledge about important rivers, lakes and mountains, introduction of non-native foods and cash crops in many countries have been brought about by strangers or foreigners. And what about modern technology, education, and systems of government we know today? We must teach and practise the naked truth that a closed society stagnates; and finally dies off (becomes underdeveloped). As strangers come into a society, they come with new ideas that may help to harness material and human resources. A supervised or properly structured open-door policy must take the place of xenophobia in all societies.

v. Good human qualities like humility, honesty, hard work, and experimentation seen in strangers and foreigners must be meticulously studied and imbibed. After all, wisdom (in its widest meaning) could be learned from others; especially from strangers and foreigners. It is on record that some of the outstanding scientists, astronauts, sportsmen and professionals in the U.S.A are of African, European, Jewish and

Russian roots. Here in lies the serious short comings of xenophobia.

vi.   We must endeavor to teach and practise the home truth; that natives or citizens inevitably need strangers or foreigners, and they also inevitable need natives or citizens. No one can be an island onto himself! There is every need for interaction between natives and foreigners so that there can be co-operation, healthy competition, and meaning; in the midst of fundamental diversity. People who are given to xenophobia must be told, rather assertively, that they stand to lose track of the on-going globalization impetus.

vii. Superiority complex that emanates from strangers or foreigners to the effect that their hosts are "mumu" and "never-to-do" leaves much to be desired. Strangers and foreigners must show respect and understanding for the ways of life and human qualities of their hosts without reservation. Such approach surely fosters mutual respect and fruitful co-operation.

THINK ABOUT THIS

"After all, wisdom (in its widest meaning) could be learned from others, especially from strangers or foreigners. Why then should a present day republican citizen think that his fellow citizens are slaves or inferior to him because of primitive history?"

.... It is reactionary to live in the past!

Be a reformer, buy more copies of this book and give to your loved ones. In this way, you will help build a better society!

PART 2

HEALTH IS WEALTH: THE 4 KILLERS TO BE WATCHED BY THE YOUTH

- Tobacco (Nicotine)
- Alcohol
- Narcotics
- HIV & AIDS

INTRODUCTION TO HARD DRUGS

Hard drugs are harmful drugs that have the capacity to create addiction or dependency in their users. In this part of this book I shall use the term "hard drugs" to generally describe narcotics, nicotine (tobacco), and alcohol. I shall treat these three examples of hard drugs under three chapters. These hard drugs may appear harmless and useful until their use is abused. Drug abuse may be described as "a constant and general uncontrollable use of one or a combination of drugs without a doctor's prescription or supervision". The abuser of hard drugs often reaches a stage where his appetite for a particular drug or a combination of such drugs becomes insatiable.

This strong or uncontrollable desire is usually the result of physiological and physical forces. At this stage, the abuser is described as a "drug addict" or "drug dependant". (Henceforth, I shall prefer the term drug dependant to drug addict throughout this text). This, dependence is a combination of uncontrollable physiological and physical craving for a drug or drugs. Ordinarily, drug abuse and dependence are unacceptable (bad) and dangerous. It does not matter whether the drug involved is caffeine, chloroquine or one of the essential body vitamins or minerals. Thus, over-feeding (excess intake of food) is as bad and dangerous as the abuse of conventional poisons. Drug abuse is no more a problem of the slum (ghetto) population, or the poor and the neglected. Even middle class people (the rich, the highly educated, and the privileged) are neck-deep in an alarming drug abuse and dependence.

Hard drugs (narcotics, tobacco, alcohol) directly cause and aggravate a catalogue of sicknesses and diseases. However, hard drugs do not directly cause crimes; but rather, they are catalysts to crimes. They have an influencing potency to 'push' or 'motivate' their users to get into some misbehaviour that may lead to crimes.

In as must as I do not support hard drugs abuse and dependence, I do not support some of the negative solutions being sought against their influences in certain quarters either. For example, death penalty, a break in international relations, diplomatic cold wars, economic blockades and embargoes are just hypocritical and counter-productive. In fact, the production, distribution, advertising, and sale of alcohol and tobacco are more serious direct abetment of crime. The dangerous effects of hard drugs are not absolute to all countries or societies, but rather, relative to respective social and, economic settings. Let me explain: the marketing, use, and dependency on cocaine, heroin, and morphine in the so-called developed countries may be a more terrible threat to social and economic lives there than that of alcohol and tobacco. But in some so-called third world countries the negative effects of alcohol and tobacco are more lethal than cocaine and heroin.

The accelerated campaigns of national, international, and global dimensions against environmental pollution should not be at the expense of physical internal pollution of the human body. I am talking about human body pollution caused by hard drugs which lead to chronic diseases and pre-mature deaths in third-world countries, day in, day out.

These hard drugs surely raise social, medical and spiritual questions that must not be dismissed with a wave of the hand. An attendant nagging problem is the hypocritical method of selecting, defining, and blacklisting some of these drugs. Other hard drugs are treated with soft gloves because of their origin, and the coffers they enrich. For example, alcohol and tobacco (nicotine) are proudly sold in the open market, without anybody taking up arms against their proprietors, as in the case of cocaine, heroin, morphine, marijuana or opium. Who is saying cocaine, heroin, morphine and marijuana are more of dangerous drugs than alcohol and tobacco (nicotine)? Like the proverbial ostrich, the proprietors, shareholders and governments of the tobacco industry hide behind 'transparent and soft' warnings (or is it high-tech advertisements?). Just consider these proclamations 'against' tobacco: "The Surgeon-General (Ministry of Health) warns that tobacco smoking is injurious to health: tar 15mg, nicotine 1.3mg" and "TOBACCO SERIOUSLY DAMAGES HEALTH Source: EC Council Directive 89/622/EEC".

Is tobacco as dangerous and lethal as cocaine, heroin, morphine, opium and marijuana? If yes, then, why the dilly-dally tactics? Who is fooling who? Now let me ask: is there any social, economic, and spiritual justification for manufactures, shareholders, and governments to kick against profits and taxes from cocaine, heroin, marijuana and morphine only to accept same from tobacco and alcohol? Whatever is your answer: my second question is, why? Can somebody out there please help me to ascertain the social, economic, and spiritual blows tobacco and alcohol are dealing to poor and unsuspecting third world countries, as compared with rich and highly industrialized countries?

I strongly advise the so-called third world countries (or is the South?) to use all PEACEFUL MEANS to reject and resist the production, distribution, advertising, and sale of alcohol and tobacco with all godly zeal; just as the so-called developed countries are doing against other narcotics.

Individuals, the clergy, imams, khadis, NGOs, professionals and governments: who is on our side? To both the "developing" and the "developed" countries I say: CAVEAT EMPTOR! Let the producer, seller, buyer, and consumer beware!

CHAPTER 14

TOBACCO (NICOTINE)

The Nature Of Tobacco (Nicotine)

Nicotine is the major lethal chemical in the leaves and smoke of tobacco. This chemical has damaging effects on vital organs in the human body. It is another misery, chaos, and death motivating drug. Yes, it has very degrading social, economic, spiritual, and physical consequences on the life of its users. Tobacco is usually smoked (cigarettes and cigar) chewed (the processed leaf and powder) or sniffed (the powder) by its users.

Causes Of Smoking Tobacco

i.   The youth, and in some cases younger children, get into this dangerous habit of smoking, chewing and sniffing tobacco through the bad examples of others. As they see their friends, school mates, relations, and even parents practise it with impunity, they become enticed to it.

ii.   Curiosity may "push" people to try their hands on smoking. As they see proficient doctors and nurses, creative engineers, intellectual teachers/lectures, famous film stars successful businessmen, astute politicians, logical authors and the "holy" clergy smoke proudly and fashionably, they mistakenly imagine that the potency of tobacco contributes to the qualities they admire in these elites. They blindly follow these 'models' to smoke. We often hear people argue: "If smoking is so dangerous to health, why then do doctors and other medical personnel smoke?" Their curiosity thrives on fallacy!.

iii.   Also the false belief that tobacco is a "problem-solving stuff" often mislead people into smoking. Thus, those with physical, mental and social problems resort to smoking for solutions. Specifically, frustration, pain, lethargy and nausea are some of the problems that lure people into smoking.

iv.   Films, books, periodicals, theatre and aggressively manipulative adverts that "promote" smokers as "champions" or 'heroes' often brainwash teenagers (the youth) indirectly. They create false impressions and imaginations about smoking in the minds of teenagers.

v.   Boredom and loneliness are also principal causes of smoking. The youth who want to be "kicking and moving" often resort to tobacco to shake off boredom and loneliness. To them, tobacco 'warms' them into action and imaginary fellowship.

vi.   Over-ambition is also a force to be reckoned with when discussing causes of tobacco dependency. A burning desire to excel, at all cost, in music, drama, fine art, and academics pushes the youth into tobacco smoking. They find extra energy in the pep effect of tobacco.

Effects Of Using Tobacco (Nicotine)

i.   Nicotine, the principal chemical in tobacco causes high respiration rate in the body; which has adverse effects (pressure) on the lungs and the heart (cardio-complications). For example, high blood pressure and faster heart beats are dangerous to one's health.

ii.   Gastro-intestinal problems that result in nausea and vomiting are associated with tobacco smoking.

iii.   Smoking reduces appetite and consequently causes loss of weight; which is the result of malnutrition.

iv.   Nicotine causes almighty cancer; especially in the lungs, mouth, larynx, oesophagus and bladder.

v.   Tobacco causes severe damage to the body tissue. Thus, miscarriage (abortion), premature births and deaths among very young babies could be caused by it.

vi.   Chronic bronchitis and other respiratory diseases are usually traced to tobacco consumption. It is on record that some $368 billion (368 billion U.S. dollars) was paid as part settlement for the treatment of tobacco-related diseases in 40 states in the United States of America by cigarette makers.

NO WAY FOR SMOKING

Why are weak
And panting for breath
Even in free and plenty air?
Why is your blood weak in your body
Not able to support your heart
And you lose weight everyday?
Why are your eyes blood shot
And you go about with body odour
That makes you the odd-one –out?
Why do you hide your black finger tips
And your teeth while you smile?
If you are ashamed of yourself
You embarrass others too!
Useless smoking will kill you quick
Oh, my dear smoker
Cigarettes, marijuana, and all smoke
Will soon smoke you to death
Why not decide to day
And say boldly:
"No way for smoking"!

Be a reformer, buy more copies of this book and give to your loved ones. In this way, you will help build a better society!

viii. Tobacco consumption gives rise to ulcer of the liver and its attendant complications. In Britain, the British Medical Association said it costs $990 million (990 million U.S. dollars) to treat tobacco-related diseases yearly.

ix. Tobacco smoking, sniffing and chewing are detrimental to personal cleanliness. Tobacco gives a permanent embarrassing body odour which is not easy to eliminate completely.

x. Tobacco consumption is a sure economic drain pipe. It can force one into pilfering (among the unemployed and low-income workers) and petty debts that are quite disgraceful. This is because as smokers waste money on tobacco itself, so they do buy mouth-washes, perfume and drugs to combat the embarrassing legacies of tobacco. Smokers always have a bigger but unnecessary budgets.

xi. Decent and reasonable people tend to avoid tobacco users. Smokers and snifters of tobacco are often considered as ruffians and happy-go-lucky fellows. Smoking is seen in some quarters as something for the non-prudent and the not-far-sighted persons.

xii. The death rate among tobacco consumers is seventy per cent (70%) higher than that of tobacco-free people. Tobacco causes cardiac vascular problems which often lead to seizure (heart attack) and final death. It has been scientifically computed that each stick of cigarette, cuts one's life by eleven minutes. Therefore, a packet of twenty sticks of cigarettes reduces life by three hours forty minutes (3 hrs, 40 mins). Accordingly, a carton of two hundred sticks of cigarettes shortens life by one and a half days. Three hundred million (300 million) youth are tobacco dependent (source: WHO).

Corrective Measures For Tobacco Smoking

i.   It should be understood that nicotine is a habit-forming (dependency-induced) drug. Therefore, corrective measures must involve gradual withdrawal strategies.

ii.   All appearances and the scent of tobacco (even from close associates) must be removed from the withdrawing smoker. He should be practically encouraged to have a strong determination to quit smoking.

iii.   Films, books, magazines, theatre and manipulative adverts that 'promote' smokers as achievers, and smart follows must be prohibited. Instead, the evil effects of smoking on the youth must be highlighted through films, books, magazines, and voluntary personal testimonies of victims.

iv.   The tobacco-dependent should be given psychological counseling to the effect that tobacco is not a problem-solving stuff. In fact, it is not a magic wand or escape route for man's mental, social, economic and spiritual problems. Rather, it causes and multiplies all types of human problems.

v.   There should be a concerted campaign by the Central or Federal, State, and Local Government administrations to use their education, health, and public enlightenment outlets against smoking. Simple and practical pamphlets, handouts, lectures, demonstrations, jingles, free counseling, treatment, and rehabilitation of tobacco dependants must be incorporated into these campaigns.

vi. Fervent and continuous prayers, and the holy Word of God against smoking could be directed to the nicotine-dependant.

vii. Anti-Smoking and Tobacco-Free Clubs could be formed or sponsored by concerned citizens and bodies, in primary, secondary, tertiary schools, and in religious congregations.

viii. Smokers of tobacco should be encouraged to use mouth washes and anesthetics under the supervision of medical experts. For instance, lobeline is an effective alternative to nicotine. Also, nicobrevin is a useful anti-smoking drug.

ix. In severe cases, the dependant victim must be hospitalized for intensive treatment and rehabilitation. This may require some time and money, but it is worth it.

x. As in the cases of cocaine, opium, morphine, heroin and marijuana; tobacco must be banned completely. The international communities that support the total ban against narcotics must, as a matter of urgency, spearhead and sustain a global ban on tobacco. The present 29% taxes in the United States of America, 70% taxes in the United Kingdom, and even over 70% taxes in some European countries imposed on tobacco are nothing but shocking acts of hypocrisy. They are just untenable! Again, I ask: does any government or individual have the moral justification to benefit from taxes or profits accruing from the consumption of deadly tobacco (nicotine)? Tobacco must be banned, like cocaine, morphine marijuana, heroin and opium.

xi. It is rather sad and difficult to understand why as the developed economies like Britain and United States of America are hiking tobacco taxes, many poor and disease-infected third world countries are cutting down same. Some of these poor countries with the most shocking low life expectancy and human development indices are even inviting tobacco companies that are closing shop in America and Europe to come in and help kill their citizens faster with tobacco (nicotine). What a difficult wisdom and bogus economics! This attitude must change through international co-operations.

I do not intend to deride the poor countries that are guilty in this reference; but to provoke them to good works. It is functional wisdom for the third world countries to imbibe the applied economics and morality which the rich and developed countries exemplify in this context.

On the 15th of March, 1998, the Sunday Champion (published in Nigeria) published this news extract. Read on:

"Clinton endorses tobacco bill"

"President Bill Clinton (of America) has endorsed a bi-partisan senate tobacco bill that aims to slash teenage smoking by half within three years.

The senate bill, offered by Democrat Tom Harkin of Iowa and Bob Graham of Florida, and Republican John Cafee of Rhode Island would raise cigarette prices by 1.50 dollars a pack over two years and cost the industry around 600 billion dollars ($600bn.) over 25 years. Billions of dollars in additional penalties could be imposed if the companies do not meet youth smoking targets.

Tobacco industry observers said that would nearly double the 368.5billion dollars ($368.5bn.) contemplated in the industry-backed settlement plan reached on June 20, 1997.

The Kids Act would cut tobacco use by kids in half over the next three years through aggressive and comprehensive reforms. That's the sharpest and fastest reduction achieved by any bill proposed to date. Unlike the settlement proposal, it allows all kinds of law suits against the industry but caps legal pay out at eight billion dollars ($8bn) a year.

Clinton has also supported democratic tobacco initiatives in the House of Representatives and senate and said he is open to any bills that meet his five objective on tobacco" (quote ends).

My dear reader, do you see morality and applied economics flowing together? The ball is in your court!

xii It is believed that a stick of cigarette soaked in honey, and dried, if smoked by the dependant could help him/her quit smoking for ever. Over to our medical and science experts!

THINK ABOUT THIS

"It is rather sad and difficult to understand why as the developed economies like Britain and United State of America are hiking tobacco taxes, many poor and disease-infected third world countries are cutting down same. Some of these poor countries; with the most shocking low life-expectancy and worrisome human development indices are even inviting tobacco companies that are closing shops in America and Europe to come I tobacco (nicotine). What a difficult wisdom and bogus applied economics?

... What future do we dream of? Who has failed in his responsibility?

> *Be a reformer, buy more copies of this book and give to your loved ones. In this way, you will help build a better society!*

CHAPTER 15

ALCOHOLISM

The Nature Of Alcohol

Gin, wine, beer, ordinary fermented fruits and beverages (burukutu, pito, palm-wine, etc), all contain varying percentages of alcohol. Alcohol is the intoxicating chemical substance found in these things mentioned above, as a result of fermentation. Gin, wine and beer (whether local or otherwise) often have higher alcohol contents, depending on the mode of brewing. Alcohol causes detrimental psychological and physical effects on the human brain, the nervous system, the blood, and other important body requirements. And this is more alarming since its absorption in the human body system is even faster than that of ordinary water. Alcoholism may be periodic or continuous. Either type is bad, and must be discouraged without reservation. A person with uncontrollable habitual and excessive drinking life-style is described as an "alcoholic" or "alcohol-dependant".

Causes Of Alcoholism

The causes of alcoholism are basically the same as that of smoking.

Effects of Alcoholism

i.   Alcoholism causes serious psychological disturbances in the brain, and then, in the entire body. For example, it leads to a vicious cycle of false happiness, tension, anxiety, and depression which is quite difficult to break.

ii.   It causes malnutrition and its resultant loss of calories. And malnutrition makes the sufferer very vulnerable to sicknesses and diseases. Thus, drunkards usually complain of headache, cold, fever, nausea, vomiting and such disease symptoms. They are usually weak and under-weight people.

iii. Alcohol, like tobacco, is linked with gastro-intestinal disorders like nausea, vomiting and stomach purging. This may in turn affect effective digestion and absorption of food necessary for body growth.

iv.   It also causes serious liver damage which can be chronic and difficult to repair. This leads to blood vomiting and possible death. Hepatitis is closely linked to alcoholism.

v.   Loss of muscular control, which is the direct result of tissue damage in the brain is usually traced to the excessive consumption of alcohol. This causes shaking of the hands, legs, and head.

vi. Alcohol causes reduction in the sensitivity of the nervous system, and also, dulls the higher functions of the brain. It is a kind of narcotic analgesic whose usage must be carefully controlled under expert supervision. Alcohol suppresses pain. Thus, its abuse and dependency, like the narcotics, account for a higher percentage of mental derangement cases.

vii. Even on a milder scale, its reaction on the brain causes embarrassing hallucinations. For example, a drunk bursts into foolish talk, barbaric shouts, unexpected laughter, costly jesting, and even unprovoked wailing, without any accountable reasons.

viii. Consumption of excessive alcohol results in impaired brain and limb co-ordination (psychomotor disabilities). Drunks easily and often fall or get involved in accidents because there is always a chance of time, space, and distance miscalculations in their minds. Many accidents in the home, factories, offices, farms and on the motor-ways are caused by the influence of alcohol.

ix. Disgraceful and ego-deflating behaviour and appearances cause the alcoholic to lose friends any sympathizers. Alcoholism breeds a nuisance, who decent and responsible fellows shun.

x. Drunks can even urinate and soil their clothes with faeces in public. Alcohol can make one sleep in the gutter, by the road side, in public parks and gardens, and even in the market place, without shame nor fear.

xi. Alcohol consumption is always a monetary wastage. The desire to drink always pushes people to overshoot their budget ceilings and consequently land in debts.

GIVE PEACE A CHANCE

Who have woes?
The drunkards
Persons without temperance
The very salves of alcohol
The whipping boys / girls or cruel drink

And what are their woes?
From grace to grass!
Their lots are shame and disgrace
Their lots are poverty and debts
Men and women of reproach
Disgraced and disowned by their own
Good-for-nothing, shun by all

And do they care for their woes?
No, not at all!
They live in delusion all day
Bragging and beating their chests
Not knowing that of all humans
They are the most miserable

(An extract from Words of Wisdom)
Osei Owusu-Aduomi
ISBN 978-064-559-4

xii. Excessive drinking of strong alcohol often results in instant deaths; especially among teenagers with ill-health. The death rate among alcoholics is frightfully higher.

xiii. Alcohol is a crime-motivating drug. Many people commit suicide, rape, robbery reckless driving, et cetera, under the influence of alcohol.

xiv. Alcohol, like tobacco, causes miscarriage (abortion), pre-mature births and deaths among infants. In many poor and ignorant communities, parents and guardians feed the infants on alcoholic beverages (burrukutu, pito, and palm-wine) which cause retarded growth and even mortality.

Corrective Measures For Alcoholism

i. Alcoholism must be seen as a sickness rather than a crime. Therefore, hospitalization and not police or prison detention, should be considered a very useful channel through which the problem could be solved.

ii. Psychological counseling could be employed to disabuse the minds of dependents and casual users that alcohol creates and escalates physical, mental and social problems. The effects of such problems are not easily controlled or completely eliminated. Alcoholism never solves any problems? Alcoholism is a useless and dangerous escapism.

iii. As in the case of smoking, the Education, Health and Public Enlightenment Agencies of the central or federal, state and local governments must be equipped and co-ordinated to mount anti-alcoholism campaigns in every nook and corner of the country. Such agencies must be able to assist in the formation and running of organizations like, Alcoholics Anonymous (AA), Alateen, Allied Youth, Alcohol-Free Association (AFA), et cetera.

iv. Government should encourage the formation and operations of a National Council/ Commission on Alcoholism. Adequate operative powers and general support should be given such a council/commission.

v. Drinking bars must be closed during official working hours. Some sensitive public offices and places should be declared "alcohol-free zones". For example, motor parks or transport terminals should be free from drinking joints.

vi. Also, the National Council on alcoholism and its agencies should control the alcohol contents of various drinks through legislation. Drinks with harmful degree of alcohol should not be brewed in the country or imported at all. Furthermore, prohibitive taxes must be imposed on alcoholic drinks as leverage against indiscriminate consumption.

vii. As a sickness, alcoholism could be treated with some special drugs. For instance, disulfiram could be used to treat alcoholism. The assistance of such drugs should be sought for under expert prescription and supervision.

viii. Prayers and the Word of God should be seriously and continuously considered as part of the arsenal against alcoholism.

THINK ABOUT THIS

"Excessive consumption of alcohol results in impaired brain-and-limbs co-ordination (psychomotor disabilities). Drunks easily and often fall or get involved in accidents. This is because there is always a chance of time, space and distance miscalculations in their minds. Drunks can even with urinate and soil their clothes with feaces in public. Alcohol can make one sleep in the gutter, by the roadside, in public parks and gardens without fear or shame"

.......Can we help the alcoholic? Yes, it is now or never!

Be a reformer, buy more copies of this book and give to your loved ones. In this way, you will help build a better society!

CHAPTER 16

NARCOTICS

The Nature Of Narcotics

Narcotics are hard drugs which occur naturally or in synthetic forms. Narcotics generally have the power to make their users dependant on them (addiction effect). This dependency could be psycho-tropic (mental effect) or physiological (physical effect).

Also, narcotics could be classified as either natural or synthetic. Examples of some natural narcotics are cocaine, opium, ergot, alcohol, and nicotine(tobacco). Codeine, methadone, demerol, pethidine, moramide (palfium), valium, librium, amitriptyline, lysergide (LSD), psilocyblin, phencyslidine drinaml, dexedrine, demetyltryptamine (DMT), mescaline, benzedrine, nembutal, amytal, seconal, and a host of others, are synthetic narcotics. Demerol and methadone are the synthetic brands of opium.

Narcotics are variously taken into the body system by their users through chewing, swallowing, smoking, sniffing or injection. There may be other methods of administration, but these five are well-known.

In terms of their effects, narcotics may be classified into five groups as following:

1. The Tranquillizers

These are sedatives that calm the user without producing sleep or seriously affecting mental and physical functioning. Examples are valium (in average doses), amitriptyline, librium and cannabis (in small quantities)

2. The Hallucinogens

They are the types of narcotics that cause distortions in perception, dream images, screaming (in new users), foolish imitation; barbaric shouting and unexpected outburst of laughter. Examples of this type are lysergide, (LSD), cannabis (Indian hemp, marijuana), mescaline, psilocyblin, dimethyltryptamine (DMT) and phencyclidine.

3. The Narcotic Analgesics (Opiates)

These drugs act as pain killers. They reduce the sensitivity of the nervous system and may retard brain functions. They are also called anaesthetic narcotics. Opium, morphine, heroin, demerol and methadone come under this group.

4. Stimulants (Uppers)

They are the types that give rise to higher blood flow in the body system. Consequently, they raise the heart beat and body temperature. These drugs stimulate the central nervous system for body activity. Examples of these drugs are cocaine, amphetamines (benzedrine, dexedrine, methedrine, drinamyl)

5. The Depressants (Sedatives Or Downers)

They induce a calm feeling, relaxation, drowsiness, and in large doses, deep sleep. Examples are the barbiturates like nembutal, amytal, seconal and valium (in large dose). They are usually useful for epilepsy, high blood pressure, insomnia and anaesthesia.

Causes Of Narcotics Abuse And Dependency

i. The youth get into these dangerous habits of narcotics abuse and dependency, first, by seeing their friends, school mates, relations, and even parents using them with impunity. Thus, bad example, evil association, and indiscriminate exposure lead to narcotics abuse.

ii. Curiosity is another factor that pushes the youth into the narcotics snare. As they see proficient doctors and nurses, creative engineers, intellectual lecturers, famous film stars, celebrated sportsmen and women, learned and articulate lawyers, successful businessmen, astute politicians, logical authors and the "holy" clergy use narcotics proudly and fashionably, they imagine that these hard drugs contribute to the wonderful qualities in these elites. The youth blindly follow these 'models' into drug abuse. They often argue: "If narcotics are all that bad, why do the "big men" always use them?"

iii.   The false belief that narcotics are problem-solving stuffs often mislead people into using them. Thus, those with physical, mental, and social problems resort to their use for imaginary solutions. Notably frustration, pain, shame, fear, and rebellion are some of the problems that easily push the youths into this image-tarnishing habit.

iv.   Films, books, magazines, theatre and adverts that 'promote' drug abusers and dependants as 'champions' or brave men and women often brainwash the youth indirectly. They create false impressions and imaginations in the minds of the youth.

v.   Boredom and loneliness are also principal causes of this degrading pastime. The youth who want to be 'kicking and moving' or 'exploring here and there' often resort to narcotics to shake off boredom and loneliness.

vi.   Over-ambition and pride also are forces to be reckoned with, when discussing the causes of drug abuse. An irrational burning desire to succeed in music, drama, academics, sports and other social activities often pushes the youth into narcotics.

Effects On Narcotics On The Youths

i. The use of narcotics creates an elated feeling (gay or on-top feeling), and this reduces cautious considerations. Thus, drug users are inconsiderate, callous, impatient, and generally unpredictable.

ii. Constant use of narcotics creates emotional and physical dependency. Without it anxiety, pain, self-pity, frustration, shame, fear or weakness returns to the user.

iii. Continual use of drugs causes the body to become tolerant to its effects. Therefore, larger doses are always needed to produce the same effect. Sensitivity of the body to the drug decreases as its damaging effects increase. For example, cannabis (marijuana) impairs immunity in man fifty (50) times higher than aspirin and caffeine.

iv. Both casual users and dependants often commit illegalities under the influence of drugs. They are often culprits who engage in lawlessness like fighting, rowdiness and vandalism, raping, stealing, trespass, careless driving, assault, and kidnapping.

v. Narcotics are expensive, therefore, their use is an economic drain on their users. The Readers

Digest of November 1981 had it that an ounce of cocaine sold at! £1,200 (One Thousand, Two Hundred pounds sterling); which was five times the price of gold. In 1980 the street sales of cocaine reached an alarming estimate of £16,500m (Sixteen Thousand, Five Hundred Million Pounds Sterling) in the United States of America. And marijuana (cannabis), the most widely used narcotic drug, hit £12,600m (Twelve Thousand, Six Hundred Million Pounds Sterling). In 1999 the United Nations Secretary-General, Mr. Kofi Annan, the Interpol (International Police) boss, Mr. Robert Kendall, confirmed that hard drugs had a market of about $400bn (Four Hundred Billion Dollars) a year. This amount was larger than the oil and gas trade. And it was also larger than the chemicals and pharmaceuticals business, and still, two times as big as the motor vehicle industry. "This whooping amount of $400bn, has the power to corrupt almost everyone", Mr. Kofi Annan lamented. Thus, corruption and misappropriation of money of unimaginable magnitude are caused by the narcotics business.

vi.   The use of or dependency on hard drugs is a social stigma. Consequently, those involved are looked down upon as lawless, defiant, and social misfits. In 1999 there were about 190 million drug dependants (addicts), in the world according to U.N. Source. Decent and responsible people avoid drug users and dependants, because they are always suspected of one crime or the other.

vii. Users of narcotics often end up as mental cases. A casual survey of our streets and psychiatry homes (mental asylums) attest to this effect.

viii. Overdose usage of narcotics may cause instant death; irrespective of whether the user is used to it or not. A girl whose identity was not disclosed by British security agents died of excessive intake of heroin in January 2000 in Britain.

ix. Withdrawal (discontinuous use) usually causes restlessness, weakness, depression, vomiting, sweating, sleeplessness and loss of appetite in the user.

x. Sudden and unexpected deaths, and even suicide among the youth are often linked with the use of narcotics.

xi. Specifically, the stimulants (cocaine, benzedrine, dexedrine, methedrine, drinamyl) cause excessive activity, excitation, talkativeness, restlessness, irritability, argumentation and aggressiveness. Dependants on those drugs usually have dry mouths with resultant licking of lips. Also, users of stimulants like excess sugar in tea or coffee. Cocaine ($C_{17}H_{21}NO_4$) and the other stimulants cause higher body temperature, higher heartbeat, and higher blood pressure.

xii. The depressants (nembutal, amytal, seconal and valium) cause slow body movement, impaired speech, confusion, dilated pupils of the eyes, and staggering. A sudden withdrawal (stoppage or independency) may result in fear-fullness, sleeplessness, tremor, restlessness, convulsions, and delusions.

xiii. The hallucinogens (lysergide LSD, cannabis, mescaline, psilocybin, dimethyltryptamine DMT, phencyclidine) generally cause day dreaming or trance-like mood, fearfulness, screaming (in new abusers), hysterical state (in new abusers), foolish imitations of people and animals.

xiv. The active chemical substance in cannabis (marijuana) is delta-9-tetra hydrocannabinol (THC) which causes increased heartbeat, blood pressure, respiration and body temperature. It negatively affects brain wave pattern and this leads to mental and manual inefficiency (impaired ability and agility). It also causes congestion of the mucus membranes of the eyes. THC affects the formation of sperm negatively and finally accounts for the occurrence of low sperm count. It also facilitates the incidence of lung cancer. Cannabis (marijuana) is usually smoked by its users and it gives a characteristics smoke odour and blood-shot eyes to the user.

xv. The solvents (of the benzene family, e.g. rubber solution) brand of narcotics cause running nose, blood-shot eyes, watery eyes, lack of muscular control, double vision, ringing in the ears, hallucinations, drowsiness, stupor and unconsciousness (in excess dose). They also, like cannabis, give characteristic offensive body odour.

Corrective Measure For Narcotics Abuse And Dependency

i. Before knowing what corrective measures to apply in any given situation and time, it becomes imperative for the average layman to detect roundly who is on narcotic drugs and who is not. The following descriptions and jargons can help to reveal a hard-drug abuser or one who is even remotely linked to narcotics:

a person found to possess, distribute or sell hard drugs.

a person with needle marks or fresh tattoo-like marks of blue or black spots on arms or legs.

a person with long scars over the veins of the forearms and lower legs.

a person with inexplicable drowsiness, sleepiness or tiredness so often or always.

a person often found with needles, syringe, teaspoon, cotton ball, filter tips or unsmoked cigarettes of missing filters.

a person with inexplicable absent mindedness, gazing into space, or a mimic of people and animals

a habitual absentee from home or a night bird.

a person usually found with a small piece of cloth or handkerchief with characteristics odour of dry leaf smoke or solvents.

Hard Drugs Terms

Jargon	Meaning
Ganja	Cannabis
Hashish	//
Indian hay	//
Indian hemp	//
Wee-wee	//
Mary Jane	//

Jargon	Meaning
Marihuana	Cannabis
Stuff	//
Weed	//
Bhang	//
Suma	Cannabis
Charas	//
Shesha	//
Esrar	//
Anascha	//
Dinba	//
Dacha	//
Dagga	//
Labake	Cannabis
Njemu	//
Machona	//
Thai stick	//
Soles	Cannabis
Joy-giver	//
Sky-flyer	//
Soother of grief	//
Joint	Cannabis cigarette
Reefer or log	//
Amsterdam crystals	lysergide (LSD)
Pentagons	//

Jargon	Meaning
Tickets	Lysergide (LSD)
Domes	//
Blue	
Angels	//
Window panes	//
Traffic – lights	//
Red barrels	Amphetamines
Speed	Amphetamines
Pep pills	//
Starters	//
Angel dust	Phencyclidine
Peace pill	//
Businessman's special	Dimehytriptamire (DMT)
Dross	Opium
999	Morphine
C17 H21 NO4	Cocaine
Coke	//
C	//
Snow	//
Blow	//
Toot	//
Red oil	Very potent cannabis extract
THC oil	//
Hash oil	//
Uppers	Stimulant drugs

Jargon	Meaning
Downers	Sedative drug
Shooting	Injection of drug
Chasing the dragon	Smoking heroin
Dropping	Oral administration of drug
On the nod	Tiredness effect from drug
Outfit	Drug abusers tools (needles)
High	estatic intoxication
Pothead	Cannabis dependant
Turn on	To smoke cannabis
Tighten up	//
Zig zig	Paper for rolling cannabis and cigarette.

ii. For any corrective measure to be effective, hard drugs abuse and dependency must be seen in a more scientific perspective. It must be considered by individuals, NGOs, and government agencies as a medical problem; and not a criminal one. It is a sickness, rather than lawlessness!

iii. Study and counsel your child or ward constantly and in details if she/he is having rampant, secret and long outings. Beware if she /he is found in the company of strange friends and often appears dirt, with bloodshot eyes, weak and rebellious.

iv. The ultimate aim for any corrective measure should be a complete withdrawal (complete independence). Anything short of this is not good enough. In severe dependency cases gradual withdrawal strategies should be applied. However, immediate or sharp withdrawal measures should be employed in a casual abuse. This is to ensure that an ordinary abuse (a mild case) does not degenerate into dependency. "A stitch in times saves nine".

v. In severe dependency cases, hospitalization (and not police cell or prison detention) is the best corrective measure to avoid further deterioration. Professional experts in medicine, psychiatry, psychology, and social welfare must be brought together for effective psychotherapy.

vi.   Effective drug alternatives could be administered under the close supervision of experts. For instance, methadone effectively takes care of the physiological craving for heroin.

vii. After effective hospitalization, there should be an immediate rehabilitation programme for the patient. This must essentially involve follow-up strategies like education, enlightenment, skills and employment acquisition.

viii. Government, voluntary agencies, and individuals must put all hands on deck to initiate and support hospitalization and rehabilitation programmes for both the casual abuser and dependant. These programmes could be directed through Borstal Homes, Youth Custody, Psychiatry Asylums/Homes, and other reformation centres.

ix.   Effective vocational guidance and training should be a vital aspect of the rehabilitation programme. These are to create or recreate social, economic, physical and psychological stability needed to make the patient useful to himself/herself, and the society.

x.   The society should be enlightened to love dependants. They should be made to have a sense of belonging, instead of feeling rejected by the society.

xi. Prayers and God's Word from holy men and women must be directed to drug abusers and dependants. All holy congregations, prayer meetings, and individuals must make it a point of spiritual duty to pray for 'friends of narcotics'.

xii. The bottom line is that no effort should be spared in banning the production, distribution and sale of ALL TYPES of narcotics (hard drugs). The countries of origin, transit and sale of hard drugs should never be a factor for banning them or otherwise. There should be no national or international hypocrisy in this matter!

xiii. Effective, pragmatic and extensive publications, campaigns, and education must be stepped up in all schools, colleges, and universities to discourage the youth from using hard drugs.

THINK ABOUT THIS

"Prayers and God's Word from holy men, women, boys and girls must be directed to all friends of narcotics"

.... My dear reader never forget to pray for, and admonish a drug abuser or dependent with the Word of God everyday.

Be a reformer, buy more copies of this book and give to your loved ones. In this way, you will help build a better society!

CHAPTER 17

HIV & AIDS

Introduction

After some two decades, the discovery of the human immune-deficiency virus (HIV), and its attendant accusations and counter-accusations about its geographical origin have given way to a medical, social, and economic thunderbolt. The effects of this shocking phenomenon have shaken the very foundation of civilization; and threatened the existence of mankind on mother earth, in unprecedented ways! No corner of the world is spared the rude scourge of HIV and AIDS. Human lives and resources are being consumed at a rate which is unabated. Here in lies the need for concerted efforts at individuals, groups, national, and global levels to stem the tide of this stubborn pandemic.

Surely, there is every hope that man will conquer HIV and AIDS some day! If the secret power of almighty cancer had been unveiled, then, HIV and AIDS will soon bow! I use this medium to console all individuals, families and nations who are counting their losses in the wave of this rude pandemic.

In the same vein, I praise and declare my support for all individuals, groups and governments who are making sacrifices to ensure that HIV and AIDS do not bring mankind to its wits end. The struggle continues! (Aluta continua!)

The Meaning And Nature Of HIV & AIDS

The acronym HIV stands for human immune-deficiency virus. A virus is a disease-causing living organism too small to be seen with the eyes. It takes even a very powerful microscope to see a virus. A virus is smaller than a bacterium. It may be 20-400 nanometres (a nanometer is 10-9 metre) (ten to the negative 9th power).

The human immune-deficiency virus is found in body fluids like blood, semen, vaginal fluids and breast milk. It destroys the natural human defense mechanism of the body (body immunity). When this is done the body becomes too weak to withstand the attacks of diseases (infections). At this stage the human body loses its natural immunity to the virus. Thus, the body has now acquired an immunodeficiency syndrome (a condition). Consequently, AIDS means: Acquired Immune-Deficiency Syndrome. With AIDS, many diseases like tuberculosis, hepatitis, gastrointestinal infections; with their attendant symptoms like headache, cough, fever, stooling and loss of weight become common to the affected person.

How Is The Virus (HIV) Contracted?

i.   The virus can be contracted through having unprotected sex.

ii.   Unscreened blood transfusion may lead to the contraction of HIV.

iii. The virus could be contracted through the use of unsterilized injection needle (syringe), shaving kits, razor blades, and other skin-piercing instruments.

iv.   Infected pregnant women could pass the virus to their yet unborn infants, or during breast feeding.

You Cannot Contract HIV:

i.   By touching, hugging or embracing a person living with HIV and AIDS.

ii.   By sitting close to HIV/AIDs patient.

iii. Through the coughing or sneezing of the HIV/AIDS patent.

iv.   By sharing toilets with HIV/AIDS patient.

v.   Sharing food or eating utensils with HIV/ AIDS, patient.

vi.   Through swimming in the same pool or place with HIV/AIDS patient.

vii. Through mosquito, bed bugs, and insects bites.

How Deadly Is AIDS?

The prevalence of HIV/AIDS and its on-slaught against precious human lives and resources differ from country to country, and probably from continent to continent. But the final devastating blow of HIV/AIDS against its victim is the same horrible eye-sore, irrespective of geographical location. In fact, I do not have the words to describe the final picture of HIV/AIDS victims, who are close to their graves, even though I have physically seen many of them.

DON'T AID HIV/AIDS

Who are you way-laying?

And why are you hiding in all corners

Calling on all comers?

Don't you know

That it's amoral

To be amorous?

Oh, my dear one

Better be careful

And come out of it

Because if you catch HIV/AIDS

You have limited aid!

Oh, don't aid HIV/AIDS

(An Extract from Words of Wisdom)
Osei. Owusu-Aduomi
ISBN 978-064-559-4

Take Time To Reflect On These Hard Facts:

i.   15-49 years age bracket people are at the highest risk.

ii. One (1) person is infected with HIV every minute.

iii. So far HIV/AIDS has no direct cure.

iv. Daily 7,000 youth catch HIV worldwide.

v.   10 million youth are living with HIV worldwide.

How To Protect Yourself Against HIVAIDS

i.   Pray and obey God's Word to stay away from the danger of HIV/AIDS.

ii. Do not engage in sex before marriage. Abstain completely.

iii. Remain faithful to your spouse (wife or husband).

iv. Do not share syringes, needles or any skin-piercing instrument with others.

v.   Do not receive unscreened blood transfusion.

vi. Use condom to protect yourself always as the last resort.

How Can Individuals, Groups And Governments Help HIV/AIDS Patients?

i.   There must be serious and consistent information and campaign against the scourge. Multi-media strategies using radio and television, jingles, advertorials, songs, drama, open-air campaigns, film shows, flyers, handbills, posters, billboards, banners, books, sermons, prayer meetings, internet bulletins, lectures, clubs, and counseling sessions must be employed on a massive scale to reach every citizen any where.

ii.   Unnecessary budget allocations to other sectors must be cut or scraped by individuals, groups, and governments so as to direct more funds to the fight against HIV/AIDS.

iii. Increased individual and corporate donations (in cash and kind) must be given to faithful NGOs to battle the menace of HIV/AIDS. Fund-raising activities could be organized for cash and materials for HIV/AIDS victims.

iv.   More new and well-equipped HIV/AIDS clinics, must be opened closer to the citizens. All existing health centres, clinics and hospitals must as a matter of urgency, have functional HIV/AIDS departments.

v.   All such health centres, clinics and hospitals must have qualified and dedicated staff for confidential and voluntary test, and counseling on HIV/AIDS. People must be freely assisted to know their status if they so desire.

vi. Those known to have contracted HIV/AIDS must be socially integrated. We must support them with prayers, God's Word, inspiration-packed discussions, intimate relations; team work in the office, factory, market, or farm.

vii. We must help them to believe strongly in life here-after. This belief will make them see themselves as lucky to have enough time to prepare themselves for heaven, through confession of sins, repentance, and faith in God. With this belief they will not lose anything through HIV/AIDS, but gain the bliss of heaven, when the time comes.

viii. Individuals, groups and governments must double their efforts in providing free and adequate anti retro-viral drugs for AIDS patients, anytime, anywhere.

There must be stronger international and global collaborations that cut across racial, religious, political, and economic compartments.

ix. There is need to give HIV/AIDs patients psychological, mental, and physiological support through consistent and adequate provisions of food, clothing, accommodation, hygienic toiletries, rest and peace of mind.

x.   There is also need for individuals, groups, and governments to initiate or support accelerated research for cheaper and more efficacious preventive and curative drugs for HIV/AIDS. In the area of drugs production, closer international and global co-operations are needed. Nobody should see himself as the sole custodian of knowledge and wisdom in this search for the survival of mankind.

THINK ABOUT THIS

"Will HIV/AIDS continue to be an unsearchable phenomena in this 21st century? This is one of the biggest challenges of the century, or is it in this millennium? Let's pray, think and work harder! God is still a Merciful God!"

....Dear reader, what part are you playing today, towards the defeat of HIV/AIDS?

Be a reformer, buy more copies of this book and give to your loved ones. In this way, you will help build a better society!

PART 3

SELECTED SOCIAL VICES THAT AFFECT THE YOUTH

- Examination Malpractice
- Sexual Immorality And Teenage Pregnancy
- Child Abuse, Human Trafficking, and Slavery

CHAPTER 18

EXAMINATION MALPRACTICE

What Constitutes Examination Malpractice?

They are deliberate attempts and undertakings aimed at having unfair advantages to pass an examination. They are short-cuts to examination success that avoid conventional methods of preparing for the examination. These unfair advantages are often sought for, and used by candidates. Sometimes too, the unfair advantage is 'bequeathed' to the candidate by the examiner, invigilator, teacher, friends, mates, and parents. Such people consider their actions as 'a help' rendered to the candidate. Their interests, which constitute an abuse of office (as in the case of examiners, invigilator and teachers) and privilege may be a direct or indirect one. Examination malpractice takes different and numerous forms, but a few common ones will be mentioned here.

i.   One of the commonest is the leakage method; where an examiner, invigilator, teacher or any examination official or their associates reveal the set questions to the candidate before the examination day or time. This is common occurrence and it is tagged "expo".

ii.   There is also the impersonation method; where someone else poses as a candidate and sits for the examination on behalf of the real candidate.

The impersonator may be a friend, or in some cases, the impersonator may not relate to the real candidate at all, but he/she does the 'work' for an agreed sum of money, a gift or a favour. Thus, this type of malpractice is often referred to as the "mercenary mission".

iii. With the "tattoo" method, all sorts of writings (the supposed answers) are written on selected parts of the body. Usually, the palms, hands and thighs are used. Writings on the thighs is employed mostly by ladies because of the difficulty in searching them freely. These writings are no made scientific in nature since they often appear in code form.

iv. Another strategy employed is the "giraffe" method. In this case, the candidate cranes out his/her neck, from time to time, in the examination-room to steal answers from fellow candidates. He/She can steal answers from those who sit in front, beside, or behind him/her.

v. Some candidates write answers on the clothes they wear in the examination hall, and even in their handkerchiefs. They stealthily unfold the ends of their clothes or handkerchiefs to copy the answers on their sheets in the examination hall. This method is code-named "screen printing".

vi. "Bullets", "missiles", ginger card" or "micro-chips" are various descriptions for answers that are folded or wrapped and smuggled into the examination hall. Such writings are often codified.

vii. A more organized and co-ordinated malpractice is what is described as "academic co-operation" or "academic alliance". In this malpractice numbers of candidates in the same hall form an alliance to help one another. Those who are good in a particular subject answer the questions fast and exchange their answer sheets with other members of the alliance. In such alliance the 'pilot members' may deliberately expose their answers to the other members that need help. Indeed, all the other types of malpractice methods highlighted in this chapter could be freely employed in an "academic alliance" or "academic co-operation". The members of such an alliance may receive money, gifts or special favours by helping other members. At times, the members give help in those subjects they know best, and in turn, receive help in those subjects they are weak. Usually, such an alliance is formed after the candidates have known their index numbers (personal identification numbers-PIN) and sitting arrangement.

viii. A more daring malpractice method is influencing a marker of examination scripts to partially award marks in favour of a particular candidate. Examination candidates, examiners, teachers and parents directly get involved in this evil. They do this on behalf of others, for personal gratification in cash or kind. Others also do it for their personal children, wards, family or tribal relations, and friends. In this case the perpetrators who proudly claim they "know somebody there" pay for their unholy business with cash, other things, or favours. This malpractice thrives on the "who-you-know" syndrome, which is an octopus of a kind. Perpetrators of this method often succeed in getting what they want.

ix.   Another more recent, but highly disturbing examination malpractice is influencing collation or issuing officials to write false grades or marks in favour of a candidate. As mentioned above, the rate at which candidates, examiners, teachers and parents influence examination officers, head teachers, principals, heads of department, faculty deans, and even class teachers to falsify final examination results in favour of their candidates is becoming unprecedented. With the advent of computer as a center of compilation and storage of confidential examination results, a new fool-proof dimension has compounded the problem. It is common knowledge that people frequently strike deals with computer room personnel of examination bodies and institutions to get grades or marks they call for. Again, this malpractice is fueled by the "who-you-know" canker.

Causes Of Examination Malpractice

i.   Teachers' laziness and recklessness with their jobs of teaching, supervision, and continuous assessment often result in students not covering their syllabus or work modules before the examinations. When this happens students find themselves in a tight corner. In their desperation some of them resort to examination malpractice to cover the lost grounds.

ii.   Students may also be lazy while teachers work hard. When parties, music, dance, sports, radio, television, video, and the rest, consume the precious study time of a student: it will be difficult for him/her to cover his/her studies effectively. In such a situation the student puts himself under unwarranted pressure. Consequently, examination malpractice becomes a ready solution to poor preparation for success.

iii. Government's irresponsibility and lackadaisical attitude towards education generally can directly and indirectly induce students to go into examination malpractice. For example, lack of teaching and learning-aids, effective school inspectors, good policies on closing and reopening of schools, good admission procedures, and prompt payment of salaries and allowances of educational workers, are just few of the remote causes of examination malpractice.

iv.   Lack of infrastructure like regular electricity, water, gas supply, furniture, tools, apparatus, conducive classrooms, libraries, and examination halls; directly and indirectly precipitate examination malpractice. Non-availability of these things could serve as enough excuse for examination officials, teachers, school administrators, and students to practice their evil trade (examination malpractice)

v.   Also, the get-rich-attitude of parents, teachers, examination officials and students leads to brazen display of audacity to ride high on this demeaning enterprise. When it comes to self-enrichment, some people easily throw morality to the winds; and use all available tactics to cheat in examinations. To them, the end justifies the means.

vi.   Sexual gratification and other non-monetary favours lure students, examination officials; and teachers into malpractice. People with promiscuous minds take undue advantage of examination candidates desperation and demand for sensual pleasure in return for "help".

vii. Solidarity among examination candidates (especially the youth) is often misused to perpetrate examination malpractice. For example, "academic alliance" or "academic co-operation" is perfected through unwholesome solidarity. The tendency for examination candidates to see themselves as "brothers and sisters" is always strong. The youth often consider themselves as one set of people sharing a common fate when it comes to examinations.

viii. Tribalism, ethnicity, stateism, and regionalism also fan the flames of examination malpractice considerably. The "we must-help-our-people" syndrome sadly blindfolds people; and they trample upon fairplay, justice, and decency with impunity. The end result could be heartless acts of examination malpractice.

ix. Increase in the number of underage students in schools, colleges, and universities is an effective cause of examinations malpractice. Many underage students are not serious with academic work (their main preoccupation in schools). Underage students do not understand the long-term objectives of their school life. They lack far-sighted focus and comprehension of human responsibilities in this world. They are easily attracted by the passing bubbles of life, (partying, singing, dancing, acting, playing, etc.) that stifle academic seriousness and its attendant sacrifice. The end result is that examinations are always a threat to them. Consequently, they try to circumvent examinations through all kinds of malpractice.

x. Unhealthy rivalry between sister institutions, examination and professional bodies, is another cause of examination malpractice, public favour, and cheap popularity they deliberately lower marking standards or inflate the marks and grades they award. They do this so that public acceptance is swayed to the fact that they are better or more considerate than the others. These are official malpractice that do not involve candidates.

xi. The over-sized premium placed on certificates, and white-collar jobs make examinations do-or-die affairs. Certificates have unnecessarily become meal tickets, therefore, people will want to go any extent, at all, to acquire them. With this unfortunate certificate psyche, there is no wonder that our hands are full of examinations malpractice.

BE UP-AND-DOING

Go to the ant
Oh, you lazy youth
Consider her ways
Work hard while it's day
Gather what you need
While the sun shines

For how long will you waste time
Oh, you careless youth?

Won't you arise
And stop wasting time?
Just a little drinking
Just a little partying
Just a little sensual pleasure
And failure shall come
The lazy youth desires good in vain
But the hardworking youth
Shall always pass his/her exams!

(An extract from Words of Wisdom)
Osei Owusu-Aduomi
ISBN 978-064-559-4

Effects of Examination Malpractice.

i. One of the serious effects of examination malpractice is the loss of confidence in, and respect for public officers. Abuse of office makes the offender partial, weak, and ineffective in the discharge of his/her official duties. This is more so when the examination leakage (expo) is the direct or indirect abuse of office by such officials.

ii. Examination leakage (expo), impersonation (mercenary mission), "academic alliance" etc. are often motivated by monetary gain or otherwise. In the final analysis, those who gain in cash or kind become corrupt. Corruption ultimately affects the society adversely. (read about bribery and corrupt in Chapter 11).

iii. Strikes, boycotts, demonstrations, protest marches, vandalism, arson, and the like by the youth are often the direct or indirect redress against examination malpractice.

Such lawlessness could be very violent when the malpractice originates from examiners, invigilators and lecturers. These wild protests always have negative consequences on individuals, institutions, and the society as a whole.

iv. Examination malpractice, breeds academic laziness, and kills self-reliance in candidates.

This is more so when prospective offenders re sure of fool-proof operations.

v. One of the essence of examination is to prove the academic or vocational quality of the candidate. Therefore, if the candidate falsely proves his quality through dubious means, the standard or quality of education is unduly lowered. What does the society benefit from a person who has Grade A1 or First Class Honours in a particular discipline but cannot perform effectively in same?

vi. Tribalism, ethnicity, stateism, regionalism and general hatred, especially in public places often lead to examinations malpractice of different shades. Thus, examination malpractice strengthens these enemies of unity and peace.

vii. One of the appalling effects of examination malpractice is the unprecedented upsurge of immorality, in public places. Especially, sexual intercourse is demanded and given, at the least opportunity in schools, colleges, and universities. "Bottom power" is a shame, a form of corruption, and of course, an abominable sin!

viii. Examination malpractice creates suspicion, laziness, and indifference in students. The end result is that positive competition is sacrificed on the altar of academic apathy.

ix. Examination malpractice that originates from or abetted by examination officials, teachers, and parents negate the authenticity of leadership by example. How can these character models compromise their integrity and sensitive social responsibility before their own children and academic juniors? When this happens the youth are hit by a moral disappointment.

Corrective Measures For Examination Malpractice

i.   Passing an examinations has become a do-or-die affair due to the fact that certificates have unnecessarily become meal tickets. The overpriced premium put on certificates must be corrected. Less emphasis should be placed on paper qualifications to reduce and eliminate the alarming incidence of examination malpractice.

ii. Government must establish and sustain more vocational, technical and technological institutions. Assessing or evaluating practical or vocational knowledge and ability is more open than writing theories. As much as possible, examinations must have more practical or verbal assessment contents.

iii. Impartial (fair and firm) examiners and examination officials must be carefully appointed to handle examinations. Even after this careful selection, they must be critically supervised to ensure that they discharge their duties with the highest integrity.

iv. Prompt, meticulous and decisive investigations must be conducted into all reports or rumours of examination malpractice. This will disabuse the minds and cool the tempers of all aggrieved candidates and officials. This will go a long way to eliminate the if-you-can't-beat-them-join-them syndrome.

v. All proven cases of malpractice against examiners, invigilator, other officials, parents and candidates must be effectively punished. Such punishments will serve as a deterrent to them and other prospective offenders.

vi. Examiners should not prove their worth by deliberately making their candidates fail their papers. Set questions must be critically reviewed to ensure that they relate to the syllabus and what has actually been taught. All unnecessary difficulties of confusing language, absurd examples and references, and punitive marking schemes must be detected and avoided. Questions must not necessarily scare or baffle the candidates.

vii. Prior to examinations, candidates must be encouraged to prepare fully. This could be done through sincere counseling and guidance, comprehensive revision of lectures and notes, and provision for other physical needs. For example, the library must be adequately equipped and made accessible to candidates, in terms of textbooks, reference books, apparatus, and other learning-aids. All distractive activities must be put off the way of intending candidates to make them appreciate the interest of school authorities, examiners, teachers and parents in their success.

viii. Adequate number of invigilators must be provided at all times in the examination hall. For example, there must be one invigilator to every 25 to 30 candidates. Where there is need for invigilators to run a shift system, this must be planned and operated without due lapses. In the examination hall, the invigilator(s) must move up and down to have a good perspective of whatever goes on in the hall. Nevertheless, such movements should not disturb the work of the candidates whatsoever.

ix. The physical set-up of the examination hall should be conducive enough to prevent malpractice of any kind. The desks or tables and chairs must be safely spaced out. Examination desks or tables must have simple design; without lockers or drawers. Laboratories and workshops used as examination halls must be scrupulously tidy. All pieces of apparatus and equipment to be used must be carefully inspected (before and after) to ensure that they do not bear codified inscriptions, "bullets" or "micro-clips". And such apparatus must be adequate enough; preferably each candidate must have one to himself or herself. Where the examination must be conducted in the evening or night adequate lighting system must be provided unfailingly. (If not, all examinations must be conducted during daytime). Interrupted power supply to equipment and lights must be eliminated, at all cost.

x. Examination fees for entry registration and resist must be affordable, so as not to scare poor candidates who because of some unavoidable circumstances need to resist or write the papers in installments. Exorbitant examination fees always create a do-or-die battle with its attendant malpractice.

xi. Failure in an examination should not be stigmatized by society. After all, an examination is not an end in itself, but a means to an end. Society (especially parents and teachers) must be sympathetic towards slow learners. Failure in a particular examination is not the end of one's academic or professional life.

xii. Academic institutions and professional bodies should necessarily emboss the photographs of successful candidates on their certificates and testimonials. This will go a long way to prevent impersonation (mercenary mission).

xiii. Before the candidates start the examination, their photographs must be taken right in the exam hall.

TIME IS SUCCESS

1. What is the time?
   What have you done?
   What have you achieved?
   Bend down and work
   Time is success!

2. Laziness breeds failure
   Don't fold your arms
   Hard work breeds success.
   Bend down and work
   Time is success!

3. Today the pains of studies
   Tomorrow the pleasure of success
   Success never comes by accident
   Bend down and work
   Time is success!

4. Never postpone studies
   Tomorrow is not your
   The worse may happen
   Bend down and work
   Time success!

(An extract from Words of Wisdom)
Osei Owusu-Aduomi
ISBN 978-064-559-4

These photographs must be critically compared with the ones submitted by the candidates when they registered for the examination. This measure can surely prove who registered for the examination, and who actually wrote the answers in the examination hall. The photograph of the person who wrote the examination is the one to be embossed on the final certificate; and not the one submitted for registration.

xv. Examination councils, professional bodies, and the examination system of schools, colleges and universities must be thoroughly investigated after every examination session to ascertain if they had done anything wrong. Thus, probity and accountability should be the watchword of all examination officials.

Preparations For Examinations

(Before Starting The Paper)

i.   Study within the syllabus. Make sure you cover enough grounds (at least, 90% of syllabus)

ii. Have a thorough revision of notes, calculations, formulae, class exercises and home assignments. Read through them slowly and pay more attention to past mistakes.

iii. Practise past papers under examination conditions. Get it right, right from day one that no "manna" shall fall from heaven. It is only hard work that can bring you success.

iv.   Be present at the examination centre, at least, 30 minutes before the official time. Avoid rushing, bumping or even crashing into the examination hall.

(In The Examination Hall)

v.   Be calm, maintain poise, and settle it in your mind, that you are going to write and pass the examination. Nothing more, nothing less! Never doubt, nor under-estimate your potentials.

vi.   Read the general instructions on the question papers carefully. Make sure you fill in details your name, your personal identification number (pin), centre name/number, gender, and any such data required.

vii. Read all questions carefully to make sure you understand them, and you can answer them. Select those you find easier, and start with them.

viii. Be time-conscious and make sure you have enough time to touch the number of questions you are required to answer. Work as fast as possible, but never be in haste to land in confusion.

ix.   If a sub-question appears more difficult to you, you may leave it mean time. This will help you to save time so that you can touch all other questions you are asked to answer. You can go back to such more difficult sub-questions later.

x.   After attempting all the question numbers required of you, take time to read through your answer carefully. Check your spellings, lexis and structure (grammar), formulae and everything. If there is need to change anything do so as neatly as possible. Remain calm, composed and obedient to the invigilator till you hand over your answer scripts and leave the examination hall.

xi.   After you have worked hard, and done all that is required of you, pray and ask God to crown your efforts with success. But never sacrifice hard work, and thorough all-round preparations on the altar of prayer! I wish you super success!

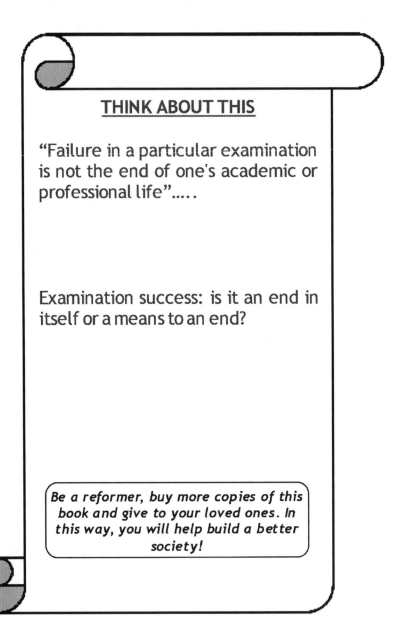

THINK ABOUT THIS

"Failure in a particular examination is not the end of one's academic or professional life".....

Examination success: is it an end in itself or a means to an end?

Be a reformer, buy more copies of this book and give to your loved ones. In this way, you will help build a better society!

CHAPTER 19

SEXUAL IMMORALITY AND TEENAGE PREGNANCY

What Constitutes Sexual Immorality And Teenage Pregnancy?

It is rather unfortunate that many people think and talk of sexual immorality as the exact equivalent of sexual intercourse (coitus). This oversight (or is it a deliberate deception?) is a dangerous cover for the extremely ugly faces sexual immorality has. People simply suggest that anything outside professional prostitution is never sexual immorality. No! I disagree with such a satanic misleading. Such a misleading comes from the pit of hell. The truth is that sexual immorality has many faces.

Sexual immorality includes and stands for anything of sexual looseness and perversion. By this, I count anything of filthy sexual language, profane sexual conversations and even conventional lectures; especially of the lopsided sex education types. It also includes all forms of careless sensual dressing, shameless body exposures, and sexy body movements. Facial expressions (body language), greetings, nicknames, hugging, and other body contacts of sensual undertones or motives are nothing but sexual immorality. Also unholy alliance, suspicious gestures, pretentious giving and unscheduled visits between the opposite genders come under the canopy of sexual immorality.

Pornography is defined as "treatment of obscene subjects, in writing, and in pictures". This definition makes it abundantly clear that pornography is part of sexual immorality. So, as wide as pornography is, sexual immorality is by far wider than both pornography and sexual intercourse put together.

Also, lesbianism, homosexuality (gay life-styles and masturbation) are typical examples of sexual immorality. Nude or half-nude modeling; strip dancing, acting and public presentation of any sort is sexual immorality. Another aspect of sexual immorality is rape. Rape is defined as "the act of committing the crime of forcing sexual intercourse on a woman or a girl". Yes, this is another ugly face of the subject matter of this chapter. It is rampant, but sadly enough, it is considered not at all as a sex crime in marriage and outside marriage, in some communities or cultures. Morality is about standards and principles of good behaviour. Anything "sexual harassment" is part of sexual indecency that needs to be condemned. Therefore, any act or attitude that drifts away from the sanctity of sex is immorality. Period!

Teenage pregnancy refers to a situation in which a girl below twenty years (teenagers are from 13 to 19 years old) becomes pregnant. Anatomists tell us that the development of body functioning may not be strictly tied to specific points in age. Thus, the physical development of the secondary sexual organs and their related enzyme functioning could be either earlier or later in an individual. However, this basic truth must never deceive anybody to overlook the dangers of teenage pregnancy. Medical experts postulate that pregnancy is always better and safer when it is prepared for. They also counsel that adulthood (20 years plus) is a better and safer period for pregnancy, all things being equal. In most cases, teenage pregnancies are accidental, and therefore, undesirable.

Causes Of Sexual Immorality And Teenage Pregnancy

i.   As the adolescents' bodies develop secondary sexual organs and their associated reactions, they become curious. Out of curiosity they imagine and wonder what all such things are to do for, or against them. Consequently, they are easily thrown into confusion. Such a situation compels them to venture into 'sexual experiments'. Pornography, first leads to sexual body contacts, which eventually shows the way to intercourse. So, curiosity opens a wide door for sexual promiscuity.

ii.   "Evil communication corrupts good manners". Yes, this is almost always true! Most people get entangled in the webs of sexual immorality through bad pieces of advice and evil association. Thus, one's immediate brothers, sisters, friends, co-workers, club co-members and co-tenants can consciously or unconsciously draw one into sexual perversion of any shade.

iii. Pornography, which is one of the vehicles for sexual immorality usually reaches people through books (especially novels), newspapers, periodicals, films, songs, drama and lectures. Such communication materials and scenes are effective in luring people into sexual perversion. Why has pornography become a sacred-cow?

iv. Covetousness and impatience make people see prostitution (both the secret and open types) as a very quick way of making money.

Such people see prostitution as a goldmine that can give them all the money they need to win the material 'competitions' they engage themselves in daily. Minus prostitution, they think they cannot wait patiently in other decent but slow-yielding occupations. Such attitudes are the breeding grounds for sensual rottenness.

v. In the area of prostitution, laziness is a strong factor for sexual looseness. Girls and women who are lazy can hardly engage themselves in occupations that require personal dedication and diligence. Naturally, they resort to prostitution which enables them to hang on others (their male patrons) or get cheap quick-money. As a first step, laziness forces such girls and women to run away form their parental or matrimonial homes, and then prostitution (secret or open) becomes the next port of call.

vi. Divorce is caused by many factors, but two are quite potent. These are uncontrollable independence and unyieldedness. Yieldedness is an unmistakable sign of true love. True love is the foundation on which marriage is anchored, without true love marriage is always shaky. Whenever a mixture of these factors becomes manifest, unfaithfulness or infidelity becomes the order. Under the cover of marriage, unfaithfulness causes secret or covert prostitution, lesbianism, homosexuality, masturbation, pornography and general sexual perversion. The "the-other-man" and "the-other-woman" syndromes are mostly caused by these deadly factors in marriage. Should the marriage finally end in a divorce, the divorcee (male or female) may quickly become a free-port for diverse examples of sexual immorality.

vii. An old wise-saying tells us that "money answers all things". Therefore, it is not surprising that poverty and need do force many single girls, and even mothers into secret and open prostitution, half-nude and nude modeling, and profane acting roles in films and drama. The dire need to keep body and soul together often leads to actions that make nonsense of sexual sanctity.

viii. Carelessness in speech, dressing, walking and association could easily open a wide door for sexual perversion of any magnitude. For example, a person who uses profane jargons, loves half-naked and transparent dressing, walks with sexy body movements and takes delight in mingling indiscriminately with the opposite gender, first opens himself or herself to sexual harassment of diverse shades. Also, he or she becomes a thorn of sexual harassment in the flesh of others.

xiii. When it comes to maintaining sexual decency, there is always the need to inform and educate. However, unrefined and unbalanced sex education materials and lectures always tend to fuel the fire of sexual looseness. Such is counter-productive. For instance, sex education topics, teaching methodology, classification (audience grouping), and follow-ups that are open to all-comers; irrespective of age, gender, sexual experience, religious background and personal choice do unconsciously legalize sexual immorality and strips it naked. Also, the use of people who are morally bankrupt, as teachers, lecturers, biologists or medical experts in sex education programmes only leads to a vicious cycle of sexual perversion. How can the blind lead the blind? How can one give out what one does not have?

ix. Another area that serves as a lubricant to the wheels of sexual immorality is the indiscriminate distribution and sale of the so-called family planning, parenthood planning, population planning or reproductive health drugs and materials. There is a big question mark over the free and indiscriminate distribution, sale and use of condoms, menstrual cycle pills, I.U.D. (intra uterus device) loops. They facilitate fornication, adultery and prostitution. Immoral medical inventions and innovations are dirty businesses and enemies of sexual reforms.

x.   Some laws (legislation) indirectly or directly influence sexual immorality negatively. Pro-abortion laws, wholesale right-to-know, total academic freedom, and some reproductive health laws and practices do relegate the sacredness of sex to the background. The end result is that what goes on before pregnancy is nobody's business; rather "unwanted pregnancies" and "population explosion" have become the darling phrases of these so-called social planners and reformers, the world over.

xi.   Research findings point to the fact that a higher percentage of new entrants into sexual immorality are taught the various evil acts by others. These "unknown teachers" are able to deliver the goods through showing bad examples to the innocent, as well as the promiscuous and experimenter. Some of the bad examples that could baptize innocent people into sexual immorality, and confirm the 'old sailors' are seducing exposure, profane conversation, immoral errands and indiscriminate crowd or group sleeping.

xii.   Most religions abhor sexual immorality to a very high degree. Any breach against such injunctions are punished by religious leaders and God.

Therefore, sexual immorality is caused by lack of the fear of God. People who do not fear, love and communicate with (pray to) God for spiritual strength to overcome the lust of the flesh easily fall into the pit of sexual perversion.

xiii. Teenage pregnancy may be the result when other forms of sexual immorality find expression in sexual intercourse that involves a teenage girl. Therefore, sexual immorality causes teenage pregnancy and its attendant woes.

Evil Effects Of Sexual Immorality And Teenage Pregnancy

i.   One of the indisputable results of teenage sexual immorality is teenage pregnancy. Whenever the sexual rascality of a teenage girl leads to an intercourse, the probability is that such recklessness will come to a head: the occurrence of an "unwanted" pregnancy. Well, whether wanted or unwanted, God has decreed that sexual intercourse should lead to pregnancy!

ii.   Many "emergency" or "unexpected" pregnancies do lead to early marriages and their attendant socio-economic setbacks. Usually such marriages are swiftly arranged for the sake of religion, moral or customary expediency. This 'baby husband' and 'baby wife' (or 'baby father' and 'baby mother') era is a remarkable contributing factor to the global social decadence which is prevalent today.

iii. Sexual immorality, in the forms of intercourse, lesbianism and homosexuality could result in sexually transmitted diseases (STDs) like almighty AIDS (Acquired Immune Deficiency Syndrome), gonorrhea, hepatitis, syphilis and genital herpes. These diseases could be deadly or very difficult to cure completely. Even before cure, they could destroy some of the reproduction organs, and cause outright impotency or infertility.

iv. Obstetric Fistula is also one of the problems associated with sexual immorality. Though it is not a transmitted disease, it is a very embarrassing deformity; which is the direct result of teenage labour (childbirth). In the process of childbirth, the teenage girl suffers dilation (tearing) of the birth canal into the anus. Consequently, the victim passes urine and stool through the same external opening. This has very serous consequences for her husband and herself.

v. Sexual immorality is a social stigma and, therefore, marks its victims as such. Men and women, boys and girls, who are sexually immoral, are not just a nuisance; but always a social risk. Prostitutes (females and males), street-lovers, and other sex addicts are usually shunned by responsible personalities, because these socially maladjusted folks are always ruffians, rascals, lust-drunk, never shamefaced, and generally, the bane of moral society.

vi. Economic adversity is another evil effect of sexual immorality and teenage pregnancy. It requires big money for food, drinking, dressing, amusement and travels to keep 'lovers' around always. Prostitutes, sexual nudist, strippers, sexy dancers, and street-lovers are in business to make big and cheap money. Since lust is highly addictive these 'sex-traders' can charge exorbitant fees for their trade. The end result is that lust-addicts are often in financial stress. They could even pilfer, gamble or steal for extra money.

vii. As mentioned before, teenage pregnancy is essentially an unexpected crisis. Such an emergency surely stretches the need for enough money for feeding, hospital charges, special clothing for mother and baby, and other incidentals. In most cases teenage pregnancy leads to poverty, especially when the husband (or is it the lover?) is not gainfully employed.

viii. Sexual immorality always works against academic concentration and discipline. No wonder, many school drop-outs are people who are sexual disasters. All things being equal, prostitution (secret or open), sexual fantasies and general libido are anathema to academic pursuit and excellence. Cases of school drop-outs and academic failure may be traced to the infectious indiscipline which sexual immorality inflicts on its victims. Such victims are always disappointed, frustrated and over-shadowed by self-pity.

ix.   Dropping out of school or academic failure could lead to loss of employment (in the case of in-service training) or difficulty in finding lucrative jobs. In this sense, sexual immorality could negatively affect the employment opportunities of both males and females. On the other hand, teenage pregnancy causes school drop-out and academic ineptitude mostly against females only. Consequently, it hampers girl-child education, employment, promotion and all-round empowerment. It always puts girls at the receiving end!

x.   When under-age girls suffer "unexpected" or "unwanted" pregnancies they experience serious body loss. This is caused by a multiple of psychological, physiological, financial and health problems. For example, shame, frustration, hunger, lack of accommodation, poverty and maternity ailments do interplay to cause body wastage. In some cases such body loss becomes permanent and quite damaging.

xi.   Also, psychological mix-ups as expressed in anger, frustration, self-pity, fear, inferiority-complex, guilt and aggression could lead to hypertension, among pregnant teenagers. Medical experts advise that hypertension during pregnancy is a dangerous maternity problem that needs to be handled promptly and conclusively.

xii. As mentioned before, obstetricians tell us that enzyme functioning that facilitates reproduction in the female develops much later than the development of the secondary sexual organs. Therefore, the appearance of breasts, pubic hair, and menstruation are not enough guarantee that the girl can soon after go through childbirth successfully. There is always the need for a well-developed enzyme reaction system to facilitate abdominal and pelvic bone contraction and expansion. In fact, a well-developed reproduction enzyme reaction system does a lot more to enhance safe child delivery than what are mentioned here. Therefore, early teenage pregnancy, without a well-developed enzyme reaction order, often results in prolonged labour, and even maternal mortality.

xiii. Induced abortion, miscarriage and child dumping are some of the undesirable consequences of sexual immorality and teenage pregnancy. These do cause serious body damage, and even premature deaths to both mother and child. In fact, deliberate abortion and child dumping are heinous crimes and sins against God and man.

xiv. Separation, divorce and broken homes are part of the ugly features of sexual immorality and teenage pregnancy. When these social vices bring about a hurriedly-arranged and baseless marriage, there is always an unwilling wife or an unwilling husband. In such a circumstance, the marriage exist in its shadow only, and fizzles out completely with the slightest upset.

xv. My dear reader, consider these vital pieces of information from the World Health Organization (WHO):

1. 60 out of 1,000 (6%) young girls are involved in unwanted teenage pregnancy.

2. 60,000 teenagers die from pregnancy related problems and childbirth every year.

3. 4.4 million young girls undergo abortion which often results in death

4. Daily, 7,000 youth catch HIV

5. 10 million youth are living with HIV

Corrective Measures For Sexual Immorality And Teenage Pregnancy.

i. Adults should not shy away from responsible sex education. This means proper explanations should be given for the appearances of secondary sex organs and their related body functioning. This will eliminate undue curiosity that throws teenagers into sexual promiscuity. Such sex education must be wisely targeted (strict audience selection is very important), must be handled by academic or professional experts; but very necessarily by people who are not themselves morally bankrupt. These precautionary measures go a long way to reduce curiosity and its attendant confusion.

ii.   As mentioned briefly in paragraph (i) above, adults must endeavour in all situations and circumstances to set good examples for the teenagers to follow. Adults, parents, guardians, relations, teachers, medical professionals, religious leaders, and all sundry must be practically sound in sexual morality. The hypocrisy and double standards of "do what I say, but not what I do" must be done away with totally.

iii.   All efforts must be made to shield teenagers from evil associations and profane communications. Teenagers must be necessarily taught and practically encouraged to dissociate themselves from people of dubious character. This must be done with all apostolic zeal, irrespective of who or what such 'moral nuisance' may be to the innocent teenager. Moral rectitude must never be sacrificed on the altar of bread-and-butter, financial gains, nor academic achievements.

iv.   As mentioned earlier, sexual immorality is caused by the interplay of some negative personality indicators. Prominent among such negative attitudes and behaviour are laziness, covetousness, self-will, arrogance, and the craving for total independence. People who show signs of these must be promptly and effectively advised to understand that there is no short-cuts for success. Success comes through hardwork, patience, patience, contentment, and the attitude of give-and-take. These virtues must be stressed always as the guiding principles against the delusion of sexual immorality.

v. Pornography is a monster! Pornography is a devastating weapon in the hands of the devil! It is a weapon of mass destruction (WMD). These are hard facts that must never be toyed with. Remove pornography, and you remove the seed that germinates and grows into the mighty oak of sexual immorality. These hard facts call for concerted efforts from all quarters to denounce, fight, and eliminate the discussion of all obscene sexual subjects in writing or pictures. Books (especially novels), daily newspapers, periodicals, films, drama and lectures that claim to highlight or teach fashion, gender inter-relations, marriage life, sex appreciation, reproduction anatomy and physiology, and reproductive health; but even slightly neglect the sanctity of sex must be strongly condemned. Yes, pornography is a dangerous enemy! All hands must be on deck to fight it to a standstill, in all its ramifications. Governments, NGOs, religious bodies, and individual citizens must enact and enforce regulations for the print and electronic media to fight the rottenness of pornography.

vi. Money is not a magic wand for all human problems. Minus poverty, there are, and will still be, thousands of crippling problems that make nonsense of money-power. In fact, some problems of ill-health and social decadence are far more deadly and solution-defying than poverty. The home truth, that sexual immorality is never a solution to poverty must be preached and practised (by both females and males). Prostitution of any shade must be outlawed; and consequently prosecuted whenever it could be proved. The safest way to eliminate cobra is to smash all its eggs whenever they are found!

vii. In most cases, prostitution, and sexual perversion in general, are masterminded, abetted, and exploited by parents, guardians, teachers and employers. As suggested for Child Abuse in this book; government agencies, NGOs, and private citizens must be empowered and protected to visit homes, hotels, brothels, pleasure resorts, educational institutions, market places, and red-light streets to 'prospect' for such irresponsible adults whose activities are inimical to sexual propriety and safety. When discovered, such enemies of social orderliness must be accordingly sanctioned as a deterrent to others.

viii. The eyes are windows for the human brain, just as the mouth speaks for the heart! Yes, out of the abundance of the heart the mouth speaks for the heart! This, therefore, calls for a deliberate restraint in what is put on, how it is put on, and the motive (why) of use. Parents, guardians, teachers and religious leaders in particular, must inspect and advise the young ones on the need to cover their 'nakedness' properly. Total permissiveness (laissez-faire order) for the youth to wear anything at all, and in any manner at all, must be roundly frowned at and condemned by all. Partial dressing, provocative dressing, deliberate nudity in western modeling and native culture must be out-lawed.

ix. Related to what is stated in the paragraph above is the need to check and censor profane, irresponsible, loose, and foul language which often come through slangs, jargons, "rapping" and broken language. People should be instructed to be chaste in the selection of the words they use. Self-censorship in dressing, speech, and body movement serve as effective checks on sexual perversion.

x. Another corrective measure for sexual immorality is the discriminate distribution and supervision over the use of reproductive health drugs and materials; especially among the unmarried youth. The controversial permissive social order must not be permitted to afflict the youth, with the poisons of sexual immorality. It must be established and accepted, that putting reproductive health drugs and materials in the hands of every youth (female and male) does not solve any problem; but rather, creates and escalates uncountable social, spiritual, medical, and economic problems. Decades of pro-abortion laws, proliferation of family planning pills and devices have failed to reduce regional or national population growth rates. Regions and nations that claim to have achieved the so-called population growth control, have only afflicted themselves with uncontrollable sexual rottenness of unimaginable magnitude. "Robbing Peter to pay Paul" is never a wise solution to any problem. To eliminate uneconomic population growth rates, the emphasis MUST be on campaigns against polygamy (especially in Africa), extra marital sex, and pre-marital sex. No more, no less!

xi. The role of progressive religious bodies must be recognized, sought for and utilized in the campaigns against sexual perversion. The gospel truth that God punishes sexual immorality, here on earth, and in life-after-death must be emphasized, again and again. Even in the area of population control, the New Testament doctrine of one-man-one-wife is a more effective solution. Similarly, concerning the spread of HIV, gonorrhea, syphilis and genital herpes, morality and holiness have an edge over condoms. These more effective, morally sound, and holier principles must be encouraged and practised, instead of questionable clinical principles and devices that are fraught with a catalogue of social, medical, economic and spiritual side effects.

xii. Whenever sexual immorality results in illegitimate pregnancy involving teenagers, real problems are created. However, people around them must not panic! Neither should the teenagers involved be disowned or banished as a form of punishment for their recalcitrant behaviour. Even though we must not encourage or abet illegitimate pregnancy, once it happens, we must accept that the prevention line is crossed already. The next and best thing to do is to find a cure for the unfavourable side effects. Some of the most potent cure for the psychological troubles associated with teenage pregnancy are; acceptance, assurance, love, sympathy, and confidence. The expectant teenager must be shown extra love and acceptance. People around them (the teenager father and mother) must prove to be trust-worthy and confidential to them. This will further help them (the teenage parents) to be open and forthcoming with their problems and future plans. This makes the "unexpected pregnancy" quite manageable.

xiii. Even under pregnancy conditions, the teenage parents do need effective and sincere sex and parenthood education. These will go a long way to help them not to blame and hate one another. Accusations, counter-accusations, and outright hatred between the teenage couples reduce love, acceptance of responsibility, and co-operation towards one another, and even towards the in-coming child. Therefore, the teenage parents must be effectively and practically orientated towards their new social status as parents and couples.

xiv. Material gifts and help must be made available to people who are involved in teenage pregnancy. These should be in the form of money, clothing, food, medical care, fellowship, encouragement and prayers. Such helps will surely solve their material, financial, health and spiritual problems and bring them the peace, assurance and acceptance they need very much in a crucial time.

xv. As others rally round the teenage parents with material and health needs, they will additionally need to overwork themselves for the relief of these "new couples". Related to this solution is the fact that such couples need to have at their disposal enough time for rest. They are already under stress! Yes, rest is such an important remedy under the stressful conditions of teenage pregnancy. Rest is a psychological and health therapy that is very helpful in coping with teenage pregnancy.

xvi. Besides the boy and girl who are involved in teenage pregnancy, their respective families must necessarily co-operate with one another. There is every need for them to forgive and forget, accept responsibility, and show love and concern for their in-laws and the in-coming child. Linked with this is the fact that none of the families should use the occurrence of teenage pregnancy to sue for monetary compensation or gratification of any kind. Rather, the present and future welfare of the expectant teenager and the unborn baby must be of paramount concern to both parties. There must be strong family supports, coming out of unfeigned love, so as to avoid a broken home. After all, teenage pregnancy and teenage parenthood in an atmosphere of love, peace, and progress will surely cover a multitude of socio-economic vices. Yes, let's shout it together: "Love covers a multitude of sins!"

xvii. Professional bodies (of bankers, advertisers, retailers, insurers, estate surveyors, stock brokers, hoteliers, accountants, lawyers, doctors, nurses, educationist/educators, restaurant owners, etc.) must sanction their members who use negative "opposite gender attraction" to lobby their clientele. For example, what has a half-naked or a stripped lady got to do with the selling and buying of printing machines or general household item? If extremely negative physical exposition actually becomes a bait for attracting clients, then somebody somewhere, is callously nailing the coffins of morality and professional ethics. It is common knowledge that some banks and financial institutions have shifted emphasis from profession competence to physical attractions and moral bankruptcy when it comes to employing staff. There is every need for professional bodies to use their code of conduct instruments to fight immorality and sexual perversion, if even it involves adults.

THINK ABOUT THIS

"Any breach against the sanctity of sex is punishable by God! Therefore, people must adhere to the injunctions of God concerning sexual morality and holiness, any day, anywhere, and under any situation".......

...Now, ask yourself: when have mean pornography and deliberate shameless nudity (human nakedness) become virtues in the land?

Be a reformer, buy more copies of this book and give to your loved ones. In this way, you will help build a better society!

CHAPTER 20

CHILD ABUSE, HUMAN TRAFFICKING, AND SLAVERY

The Nature Of Child Abuse, Human Trafficking And Slavery

Child abuse includes any bad or wrong attitude or action meted out to a young person (usually one under 18 years), without justification. Very often a bad or wrong attitude or action is meted out to the child just because he/she lacks avenues for seeking redress. Whether these actions and attitudes are mild or temporary, they still constitute an abuse. An abuse against one's own child is as serious as that against somebody's.

Human trafficking in this discourse, involves using deceitful methods (empty promises for material goods, money, job, education or marriage) to persuade or force people (old and young) to move from one town or country to the other illegally. Human trafficking directed towards young people is also an aspect of child abuse. Thus, human trafficking and child abuse could be closely related. Whether the transaction and the persons trafficked (young or old) were "sold" and "bought" or not, the practice is illegal, and therefore, constitutes a sordid crime and sin. Consequently, elopement, whether as a custom or culture must be seen as human trafficking. Human trafficking invariably leads to slavery, suppression, oppression, and alienation of basic human right. It is a kind of animal kingdom justice which approves might as power. Indeed, it is an affront to human dignity!

Slavery involves making someone work hard for bad or poor remuneration either in cash or kind. Whenever child abuse finds an unfortunate expression in human trafficking, slavery becomes a regime. Both the youth and elderly people could be slave drivers. Therefore, it is always useful to tackle these three social vices as inseparable bedfellows.

Specifically, the following are some of the naked and mind-boggling aspects of child abuse, human trafficking, and slavery!

i. Cruelty against children, especially in the form of unjustifiable molestations, scolding, taunting, and beating are very disturbing abuses.

ii. Another blood-curdling and extreme cruelty against children is intentional killing. Some adults willfully kill children for money, religious sacrifices, traditional vows and spiritual powers. Any request for human blood and physical parts, quickly switches the adult's mind to those of the child. In times of war, famine, and other natural catastrophes children are willfully abandoned or killed to make escape easier for the adult. Under refugee conditions, children suffer and die most.

iii. Illegal or improper adoption of a child constitutes an abuse. The child has every right to have, and be with his/her biological parents.

iv. Negligence and inadequacy in providing the physical and physiological needs of a child; like average accommodation, education, clothing, feeding, healthcare and safety, at all times, is a flagrant abuse. Even it times of economic difficulties, human and natural catastrophes (fire, flood, earthquakes, tornadoes), below-average provision of these needs is an abuse that needs immediate correction.

v. Another face of child abuse is the refusal to give the child modern education and vocational training, at least, up to senior secondary school level. Any deliberate attitude or action of parents or guardians that forces a child to drop out of school is as bad as any physical cruelty against him/her.

vi. Early marriage, especially in the case of girls; for economic, social or religious reasons is reactionary, and therefore, constitutes an unpardonable abuse. It inflicts direct ill-health like (Obstetric Fistula), on the girls, forces them out of school, and multiplies their socio-economic problems in adult life.

vii. Sexual exploitation, in the forms of rape, incest, foul body contacts, caressing and indecent touching of boys and girls are shameful child abuses. Even introducing children to facial expressions, filthy and profane language (love songs, nicknames) of sensual undertones constitute an abuse. These things ultimately lead to sexual looseness and perversion among children.

viii. Today, adults do frown at, and reject tribal marks (facial marks or tattoos) because of their awareness of the dangers such things impose on them. But surprisingly, they inflict same on children. In the same vein is the abusive culture of female genital mutilation (FGM) imposed on ignorant and innocent girls. These abuses are just callous!

ix. One of the most complex and widespread forms of child abuse is the misuse of child-labour. Child-labour has been defined as the employment of girls and boys when they are too young to work for hire, or when they are employed at jobs unsuitable or unsafe for children"

x. A common way of using child-labour is where children help their own parents or guardians with chores in the house, farm, or market. The understanding should be that the child is willfully contributing or helping to provide the needs of the family. Anything "unsuitable" or "unsafe' is not good enough. For example, any act or attitude that employs force against the child for his/her labour is evil. Now, get me right: I am not against training the child to be hardworking, a labour-lover, and to contribute his/her quota to the family pool. I rather advocate that such training and exposure must come through positive, rewarding, and appreciation methods that are devoid of threats, armtwisting and brutal force Secondly, children may willfully approach employers of labour to work for wages or salary. In this case, if children are assigned to jobs unsuitable for their ages, it is still an abuse, irrespective of how much they are paid. Also they should not be underpaid or made to overwork just because they are children and cannot seek redress. Another aspect of abuse in this second case is making children to work in over-crowded or unhealthy environment, sleeping in their work places (in cases of the poor or orphans) and neglected in potential health hazards.

Thirdly, some children are "given out" (sold into slavery) as domestic, commercial, or farm helps for monetary gain or otherwise by their parents or guardians. Such parents or guardians have no justification whatsoever, as long as the persons they have "given out" for labour are children. And it becomes a case of double abuse when their Alhaji, Mallam, Master, Oga, Auntie or Madam misuses them. Slavery in all its ramifications is improper, sadistic, illegal, and inhuman!

A fourth and more subtle way of tapping child-labour is in the area of public entertainment. As the child amuses himself/herself, attracts public attention and gifts, he/she forgets completely that he/she is working (being a source of labour). The adult craftily makes the child overwork himself/herself, exposes him/her to physical and social hazards, and deprives him/her of commensurate income. Examples of these abuses abound during cultural festivals, commemoration days (Xmas, Easter, ld-el Fitir, ld-el Kabir, etc.) funerals, in social and night clubs, in modern advertising (TV and radio) and in video drama and cinema.

x. Using children in tribal armed conflicts, civil wars and rebellions as baby or child soldiers is an abuse that leads to human trafficking, and of course, slavery. The war against these three social vices must be surely carried to these war fronts. The onus is on the national and international agencies, and the law courts.

Causes Of Child Abuse, Human Trafficking And Slavery.

i. A major factor that works against children in the areas of abuse, human trafficking and slavery is vulnerability. Children are weak and helpless because they lack the wisdom, experiences, boldness, money and at times the physical strength to protest, complain, and seek redress against these inhuman acts. These characteristics of children make it easer for them to be abused, deceived through trafficking and finally dumped in slavery.

ii. Adults take undue advantage of these characteristics mentioned in (1) and unleash unbridled callousness, sadism, and totalitarian commandments on children. Usually such Oga, Alhaji, Mallam, Madam, Master or Auntie hides under the guise of "correction", "punishment", "training" and "discipline", which they will NEVER allow anybody to look into. Where are the checks and balances in extreme child upbringing principles? It looks like there is none! Oh, what a pity!

iii. Linked to that cause is government's complicity. I am aware that various governments are signatories to international treaties and conventions on summary cruelty to children. However, I find that some have neglected to give detailed assessment, expansion and classification of these vices, as they apply to their specific customs, culture, religion, economy and national orientation. Why are governments now neck-deep in organizing or sponsoring beauty pageants, where girls below eighteen years (or even above) are compelled to strip naked under the prowling eyes of men (including parents) of all ages, status, mandate and mindset? In fact, I have accidentally witnessed a beauty pageant in a nursery-primary school before. For the avoidance of doubt, and for the sake of clarity, I quote the definition of BEAUTY PAGEANT or BEAUTY CONTEST from the Oxford Advanced Learners Dictionary: "a competition for young women in which their beauty, personal qualities and skills are judged". Now, let me ask: Is it necessary for somebody to strip naked before-her beauty, personal qualities and skills are judged? When has shamefacedlessness become an ideal personal quality or skill?

iv. Again, the insincerity and non-challant attitude of some governments and their agencies indirectly serve as a cover for child abusers, human traffickers and slave drivers. A situation where documents, literature, or information handbills that expose and denounce these vices are sacredly kept in the storerooms of the government press, in the national archives, or even in the museums, leaves much to be desired. Radio and television campaigns against child abuse, human trafficking and slavery are seasonal, short-lived, and far in between. These vices are hardly seen as epidemic not to talk of pandemic! Consequently, actions directed against them are lethargic and dragging-of-feet.

v. Lack of awareness and sustained action from government quarters have directly blurred the vision of non-government organizations (NGOs), business houses, and public-spirited citizens to join the crusade against child abuse, human trafficking, and slavery. There is widespread apathy towards these vices; and that is part of the reasons for their seeming invincibility.

vi. National or territorial (regional/sectorial) economic fluctuations or/and complete failure usually cause depression and inflation. These further result in inefficiency in socio-economic infrastructure and its attendant lower standards of living. Under such socio-economic hardships, child abuse, human trafficking and slavery become the order of the day. Thus, bad or weak economy is a breeding ground for these vices.

vii. Divorce, permissive and broken homes often create parental complicity. Single parenthood, problematic step-father and step-mother relationships easily drive children away from home prematurely. The end result is abject need for the basic welfare of the young ones. The child painfully submits himself or herself to all shades of abuses, migration, and slavery. And when unfortunately death takes away the parents, only God knows what becomes the fate of the orphans!

viii. Greed, unbridled love for money and material things, on the part of adults make them stop at nothing in exploiting the unsuspecting young folks. On the other hand, the same greed and get-rich-quick mindset make children and youth (both male and female) fall victims to abusers, human traffickers and slave merchants. Covetousness can blindfold people till they fall into the pit of evil experiences.

ix. Lazy people fold their hands all day long. On the contrary, they expect "manna" to fall from heaven for their continual satisfaction. Such people are usually complainers, insatiable and excuse-givers, who will, at the slightest opportunity, jump into any moving wagon, without minding its destination. Thus, unreasonable and uncalculating people see any crook or charlatan as a messiah who will take them to the promise land. No wonder even adults, in their right senses could submit themselves to be trafficked into slavery.

x. Savage customs, rituals and cultural practices that discriminate against people and peg them at the receiving end, make them run away from 'home'. When peace, satisfaction, and a sense of belonging elude people continuously, they may leave their family homes, ethnic land or native countries without careful preparation for eventualities. Consequently, they jump into the unknown only to find themselves in the hands of exploiters. Similarly, counter-productive religious dogmas and barbaric practices like early marriage, forced marriage, imposed withdrawal from school, forceful incision of tribal marks, female genital mutilation (FGM), the caste system and illegal banishment or restrictions compel people to seek succor elsewhere, only to land in exploitation and slavery.

xi. Illegal and improper adoption of young people often result in abuses, human trafficking and slavery. Improper adoptions make the adopted child be at the mercy of his/her guardians, and consequently he/she loses the natural love and affection he/she deserves.

xii. Unproductive or non-functional education system produces people who are always dependant on others. When people are not self-reliant, they are vulnerable to exploitation, especially human trafficking and slavery. Such an education system makes survival of the fittest a pre-occupation and a normal order.

xiii. Armed conflicts, civil and international wars often displace people; destroy lives and socio-economic infrastructure. As a result, life becomes very difficult for the affected people and their lot could be human trafficking and slavery. Also the conscription of young people into combatants during wartime is fraught with abuses, human trafficking and forced labour.

xiv. The activities of deceitful and ghost immigration consultants often result in disgusting human trafficking and slavery. Such crooks often promise their unsuspecting clients heaven on earth, and when they finish extorting every pesewa from them, they abandon them to their fate: battle for survival.

Effects Of Child Abuse, Human Trafficking And Slavery.

i. Child abuse and its twin evils; human trafficking and slavery, create a vicious cycle of hardness, callousness, sadism, lawlessness and general social disorder. Young people who receive love and sympathy grow to be loving and sympathetic. Contrarily, those who grapple with abuses, sadism and wickedness grow to unleash same to others; because they are cast in the mould of a negative mindset.

ii.   Living and working under difficult and risky conditions make people susceptible to sicknesses and diseases. As child abuse, human trafficking, and slavery do not make prompt attention to such diseases possible; such diseases like HIV/AIDS, ulcers, diabetes, meningitis, hypertension, tuberculosis, asthma, gonorrhea, heart and kidney problems, in their worst stages are common among dehumanized slaves.

iii.   Naturally, such chronic diseases bring about premature deaths that could have been averted at earlier stages. Thus, life expectancy among people affected by abuses, human trafficking and slavery is very, very low.

iv.   When young people are abused, subjected to slavery conditions, and frequently trafficked from place to place; they end up as school dropouts. Even those who manage to finish schooling do come out as inferior scholars, who are not able to take up outstanding and rewarding professions. Such people, at best, become glorified hewers of wood, and drawers of water. They become backbenchers in the auditorium of the national economy and social life. Their lot is a vicious cycle of living below the poverty line.

v.   There is, therefore, no wonder that child abuse, human trafficking and slavery are engines that propel crimes, lawlessness and general impropriety. People who are battered by these vices wrongly seek redress through armed robbery, rape, alcoholism, kidnapping, drug pushing and dependency, arson, vandalism, assassinations and even suicide. It is a proven fact that majority of the urchins, miscreants, hoodlums, "area boys", pimps, and hooligans, who have become a thorn in the flesh of the society are the products of child abuse, human trafficking and slavery.

vi. Human trafficking, in particular, leads to costly intra-national and international brain drain. I am aware that mobility of labour, to some extent, and if it is properly guided, is a healthy exercise for the labour market, and the economy in general. But at the national level, if human trafficking (whether it involves skilled manpower or 'raw brains') is not socially and economically managed for positive results, then we create a serious misplacement of priority in human resources empowerment. When this happens, it is rather unfortunate! Thus, human trafficking and slavery adversely affect a country's human resources; such that they become unharnessed, and therefore, under-utilized. This is a serious economic waste!

vii. Also, improper adoption of young people and human trafficking lead to loss of one's national, ethnic, or family identity. Unnecessary and haphazardly planned displacements of people give rise to nagging xenophobia, ethnic or racial marginalization and dominance, and their resultant bloody clashes.

viii. Human trafficking, if not nipped in the bud, results in forceful and tragic international or regional repatriation of illegal immigrants. Whenever such repatriations receive worse reprisals, bilateral and territorial peace is badly disturbed. These have grave consequences on the enhanced social and economic order at regional or international levels. For example, the illegal aliens expulsion orders in Ghana (1969) and Nigeria (1983) dealt a terrible blow to humanity, the entire ECOWAS sub-region and humanity.

ix. Ubiquitous sexual immorality or perversion and worrisome teenage pregnancy have their roots in child abuse, human trafficking and slavery. I want to emphasize that sexual immorality or perversion; as expressed in animalistic nudity (deliberate and international stripping), commonplace sexual intercourse, profane language, seductive body movements, sensual body contacts, is fast upstaging other social vices. This is a very dangerous trend!

x. Every country in the world has its fair share of the menace of street children. Essentially, street children are abandoned children, wayward children, runaway children, uncontrollable children et al. A critical study of these children's social and economic backgrounds, always reveals elements of child abuse, human trafficking and slavery. These vices have devilish tentacles.!

What Must Be Done Against Child Abuse, Human Trafficking And Slavery?

i.   A national agency for the prevention of cruelty against children must be established with full legal backing and efficient professional staff. Where it exists already (it may be under different names) governments, organizations, and private individuals must support it in cash and in kind to make its operations super effective. It must be an uncompromising watchdog for these vices.

ii.   Adults must endeavour to champion and sustain the crusade for the well-being of young persons, at all times. Seasonal and incoherent campaigns are not desirable enough for the enormous task of protecting and salvaging young people from abuses of any kind. Any attitude or action that borders on child abuse must be vehemently avoided, discouraged and corrected without the least hypocrisy. Documents, literature or information handbills that expose trafficking and slavery must be made available, anywhere, anytime, free and in surplus quantities. Radio, television, drama and sermons must be effectively used to highlight the nature, causes, effects and solution to these monster practices.

It is only the adult who can effectively champion the cause of the young ones! A summary of children's rights, as presented here must be printed in large quantities and displayed on billboards, television and on the internet. They must also be presented everywhere, as fliers, handbills, notices, poetry, songs and even souvenirs.

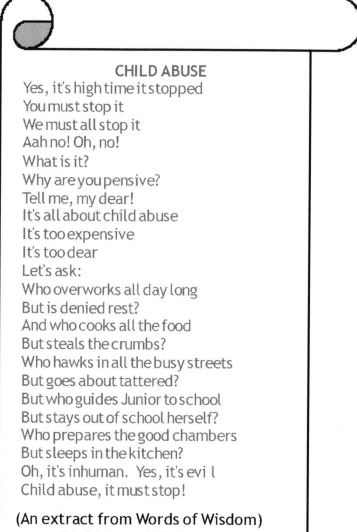

CHILD ABUSE

Yes, it's high time it stopped
You must stop it
We must all stop it
Aah no! Oh, no!
What is it?
Why are you pensive?
Tell me, my dear!
It's all about child abuse
It's too expensive
It's too dear
Let's ask:
Who overworks all day long
But is denied rest?
And who cooks all the food
But steals the crumbs?
Who hawks in all the busy streets
But goes about tattered?
But who guides Junior to school
But stays out of school herself?
Who prepares the good chambers
But sleeps in the kitchen?
Oh, it's inhuman. Yes, it's evil
Child abuse, it must stop!

(An extract from Words of Wisdom)
Osei Owusu-Aduomi
ISBN 978-064-559-4

A Summary Of Basic Children's Rights

(a) Every child has the right to life and be allowed to survive and develop

(b) Every child is entitled to a name, family and nationality.

(c) Every child is free to belong to any association or assembly according to the law.

(d) Every child has the right to express opinions and freely communicate them on any issues subject to restrictions under the law.

(e) Every child is entitled to protection from any act that interferes with his or her privacy, honour and reputation.

(f) Every child is entitled to adequate rest; recreation, leisure and play according to his or her age and culture.

(g) Every child (male or female) is entitled to receive compulsory basic education depending on individual abilities.

(h) Every child is entitled to good health protection from illness, and proper medical attention for survival, personal growth and development.

(i) No child should suffer any discrimination, irrespective of national origin, birth, colour, gender, language, religion, political and social beliefs, status or disability.

(j) Every child must be protected from indecent and inhuman treatment through sexual exploitation, drug abuse, child labour, torture, maltreatment and neglect.

iv. Children or young persons in need of care and protection (against physical and moral dangers) must be sought for, and salvaged by Juvenile Courts. In fact, Juvenile Courts and the National Agency for the Prevention of Cruelty against Children must have well-equipped and dedicated field officials who visit homes, institutions, market places, workshops, factories, and the nooks and corners of streets, to prospect for cases of child abuse and neglect. Cases so detected must be handled effectively to justify the efforts put into uncovering them. All international agencies and fora must strongly condemn child abuse without any apology. In fact, Article 41 of the International Labour Organization (ILO) convention advocates the abolition of child labour without reservation.

v. Abused children must be assigned to interested and capable foster parents, Baby Farms, Orphanages, Children's Homes, S.O.S Villages, et al. Even in theses places, probation officers must still be attached to such children to advise, assist, befriend them, and concurrently, they must investigate and evaluate the overall interest and capabilities of such foster parents or homes.

vi. Permanent employment of children below senior secondary school-leaving age must be strictly legislated against. To enforce this legislation, Juvenile Employment Bureaux must be set up in strategic locations throughout the country. These bureaux must be charged with the responsibility of detailed documentation and assessment of child labour.

vii. Governments, NGOs, corporate bodies, and private citizens must make the promotion of functional education their top priority. The educational system must be overhauled to make it labour-oriented. Lessons must be practical, down-to-earth, and capable of making students self-reliant, honest, an patriotic. School fees must be deliberately reduced through heavy subsidies. Even in private schools, governments (Federal, State, Local) must grant liberal subventions. Also superior innovations must be adopted to de-emphasize the high premium placed on mere papers qualifications. These measures will go a long way to raise young people who will not be vulnerable to abuses, human trafficking and slavery.

viii. All adoptions of young people (whether official, native, customary, tribal or whatever) must be properly documented, in line with the nitty-gritty of the national constitution, and all other laws of the land. Any law or legal inhibitions that stand in the way of proper and safe adoption of young persons must be abrogated, without the least hesitation. Even the good laws must undergo constant review and expansion till they are devoid of loopholes.

ix. Governments must effectively mobilize the citizenry to be patriotic and hard working enough, to create and sustain a buoyant national economy. A buoyant economy, if properly managed will bring about high living standards, which are panacea for abuses, human trafficking and slavery.

x. As mentioned before, barbaric and savage social and religious practices that are tagged customs, traditions, rites, rituals should never be allowed to corrupt our young ones. Governments, authentic religious bodies, NGOs and individual citizens must join their efforts together to eliminate such bad practices. By this, they can stop such bad practices from lubricating the wheels of child abuse, human trafficking, and slavery. Laws that are meant to protect the young ones must be carefully drafted to confront bad traditional practices squarely.

xi. Governments must spearhead the entrenchment of durable and humane national psyche. Religious bodies, NGOs, corporate bodies, civil societies, and public-spirited citizens must be carried along in propagating a national orientation that will play down, or eliminate the high incidence of divorce, permissive and broken homes, greed, unbridled love for money, insatiable material acquisition, and laziness. People must be encouraged to promote virtue through its practice.

xii. The need for good governance must be emphasized, over, and over again. Ruling governments, the opposition groups, regional bodies, continental unions, and global organizations and fora must persistently insist on good governance. They must be all out to sanction irresponsible government personalities, so as to avoid economy failure, political and ethnic clashes, and full-blown civil wars, which often open the floodgates for child abuse, human trafficking, and slavery. "We must all seek peace and pursue it". In this way, we shall prevent a multitude of national human tragedies!

xiii. Some economic forces make economy failure inevitable. In such instances, bilateral treaties, regional bodies, continental unions, and global organizations must be mobilized to provide a buffer (cushion effect) immediately, before these vices rear their ugly heads.

xiv. There must be regional, continental, and global common fronts against the activities of deceitful and ghost immigration and employment consultants. These enemies of the society must be confronted in the dailies, periodicals, on television, and on the internet. When caught, they must be punished in a decisive way. Also, repatriation exercises for illegal immigrants must be carried out by the host countries in humane manners.

xv. In all things, whether in child abuse, human trafficking, and slavery: both the young and the adult must be sure to have a conscience void of offence towards man and God!

THINK ABOUT THIS

'Child abuse and its twin evil, human trafficking and slavery create a vicious cycle or hardness, callousness, sadism, lawlessness and general social disorder.

Young people who receive love and sympathy grow to be loving and sympathetic. Contrarily, those who grapple with abuses, sadism and wickedness grow to unleash same to others'

......My dear reader, it's time for you to choose a right position in this matter!

Be a reformer, buy more copies of this book and give to your loved ones. In this way, you will help build a better society!